MEDIEVAL FRENCH MINIATURES

ST. AUGUSTINE AND THE PATRON SAINTS OF THE ABBEY OF MARCHIENNES. St. Augustine, *Enarrationes*, middle of the 12th century (Douai, Ms. 250, f. 2)

JEAN PORCHER

Medieval

FRENCH MINIATURES

HARRY N. ABRAMS, INC., NEW YORK

TO JULIEN CAIN

DIRECTEUR DES BIBLIOTHÈQUES DE FRANCE

LIBRARY OF CONGRESS CATALOG CARD NUMBER: 59–12874

TRANSLATED FROM THE FRENCH BY JULIAN BROWN

ALL RIGHTS RESERVED. NO PART OF THE CONTENTS OF THIS BOOK MAY BE

REPRODUCED WITHOUT THE WRITTEN PERMISSION OF THE PUBLISHERS

HARRY N. ABRAMS, INC., NEW YORK

COLORPLATES PRINTED IN FRANCE

BOOK PRINTED AND BOUND IN THE NETHERLANDS

CONTENTS

FOREWORD

THE purpose of this book is to provide a general commentary on a series of paintings. My chief concern has been not so much to write the detailed history of illumination—its outlines are shrouded at many points and much will remain obscure for a long time, perhaps for ever—as to convey a broad impression of its development. I have divided my subject into two chapters, Romanesque and Gothic: a simple and traditional division which none the less corresponds to the facts and which I felt bound to follow. The internal arrangement of the chapters, on the other hand, presented many difficulties. French Romanesque painting, from the 10th to the 13th century, was the product of a meeting of currents from a number of neighbouring regions, and it is they, for the most part, that account for its variety. But in the Gothic period, from the third decade of the 13th century onwards, the roles are reversed. France has come of age, and France calls the tune. The old pupil is the new master and everywhere the dominating influence is Paris, the intellectual centre of Europe. Once a mere importer, France is now in a position to export. The contrast between these two opposite activities must be emphasized. The Romanesque chapter is not concerned with the definition of illusory schools and their supposed development, but traces the various currents, from North, East and South, which fed the painting of the time. Without completely isolating these currents from one another, for they often blend together, it attempts to show what each one of them contributed: not always an easy task, sometimes even an impossible one, as we advance in time and the independence of France becomes established. The Gothic chapter, on the other hand, deals with a centralised art which grew by the addition of successive tributary streams, but did not change its course. It is arranged in chronological order, in so far as the chronology can be more or less accurately established.

The pictures which illustrate the text of the book and are its most important part accordingly fall naturally into family groups, depending on the chapter to which they belong. Territorial boundaries were for ever changing in the course of the Middle Ages, and I take into account only those of present-day France, since that is the only way to avoid insoluble problems. What I have written is only a sketch, the frame for which has been provided by three exhibitions organised during the last few years at the Bibliothèque Nationale; but two periods represented in the exhibitions are here omitted, for I do no more than allude to Merovingian and Carolingian art. To have dealt with the latter, which is in itself of major importance, would have taken me far beyond the limits of time and space desirable in a work dedicated to French painting alone. It would have led me on, little by little and from one allusion to the next, to deal with the whole of Europe, since medieval art knew no frontiers; and it would have rendered even more schematic a picture whose outlines are all too bare as it is.

J.P.

ROMANESQUE ILLUMINATION

FRENCH illumination began with the emergence of France herself, under the Capetians. The land of Gaul already had taken an active part in all the artistic movements that had affected the West, and in the 9th century great Carolingian schools of painting had been established on the Rhine near Charlemagne's own court, at Rheims, at Tours, at Metz and at the court of Charles the Bald; but the havoc wrought by the Norman and Saracen invasions, the slow decline of political power, and the conflicts to which it gave rise slowly but completely destroyed the accumulated wealth of artistic treasures. The 10th century, so brilliant in the East thanks to the Ottonian inheritors of the Empire, so vigorous in England, was in France the century of darkness. The renaissance began with the change of dynasty, about the year 1000, at the moment when, little by little, France herself was beginning to be reborn.

France was divided, and the task of reassembling the fragments was to call for centuries of patient labour. The central power was still weak, and the idea of territorial unity was only to be imposed under Philip Augustus in the 13th century, the Gothic century. To begin with, pictorial art was just as divided, distributed among a number of loosely-knit centres, which were linked, in large but imprecisely defined groups, only by affinities of time and place. And yet two major groups can be distinguished from the earliest times, the North and the Midi; and this too is a reflection of the political and intellectual climate. Culture in those days was the business of the clergy, especially of the

regular clergy, the monks in their abbeys; and it was transmitted by the monks through a series of exchanges which ignored all frontiers, even ecclesiastical frontiers. The instruments of this culture were the books which the monks composed and copied and which might or might not be decorated, more or less elaborately. Apart from wall painting, book-decoration was the only form of pictorial art then known, and it ranged from simple decorated initials to whole scenes with figures, which as sometimes happens in the *Lives* of saints or in the great picture-books of a later period, might invade the entire volume and even drive out the text. The history of the medieval book corresponds very closely to the history of the monks; and if painting was reborn about the year 1000, it was because the Cluniac reforms, slowly maturing during the whole of the preceding century, had by then, thanks to St. Odilo (994–1049), borne fruit in all the monasteries of France, and because, under Cluniac influence, Burgundy, Normandy, and later Lorraine and the district of the Meuse, lead by Richard of Saint-Vanne, had everywhere experienced a revival of order and prosperity. Similarly, the decline of French Romanesque painting towards the end of the 12th century resulted in part from the decline of the monastic establishments.

In the North, proximity to the countries which were then most fertile in artists—England, the valley of the Meuse, and beyond it the Empire and its Byzantine dependencies—occasioned an ever more brilliant flowering of art which reached its perfection about

the middle of the 12th century, before dying away in face of the preponderance of Parisian Gothic. In the South—Aquitaine and Languedoc—the influences of the Mozarabic culture of Spain, of Italy, of the Middle East and again of Byzantium had a different effect. It was not that two irreconcilable artistic parties were formed in France, for naturally enough points of contact were not lacking; but the two pictorial groups of the North and the Midi each kept to the end their distinct personalities. This distinction matched the differences of language (langue d'oïl, langue d'oc) and even of law (common law, Roman law), and the corresponding differences of customs and taste. The picture presented by French Romanesque painting is, then, a diptych.

We must begin by defining what it is that distinguishes the two wings of this diptych, and what it is that unites them.

The decorated initial, so characteristic of Romanesque illumination, is a medieval invention, and it differs profoundly as between North and South. The antique world knew only the simple capital letter, which was sometimes employed to emphasize not only the beginning of a book or of a chapter, as we do, but the first word of a page, or even the end of the word if it was divided. The appearance of the page as a unit of script meant more to the scribe than the text it contained. The earliest decorated initials are perhaps as old as the 6th century, and they arose, under conditions not as yet closely defined, from the shape of the initial letter itself, which suggested to the scribe some sort of figure: a bird, a fish (Fig. 1), later on a human face. At the end of the 8th century, when closer contact was established between the descendants of the barbarian tribes and the world of Mediterranean art, decorators extended to the initial, itself increasingly heavily ornamented, the imagery with which, after the Late Antique fashion, they were beginning to illustrate their works: narrative scenes of subjects provided by the text, or scenes of pure fantasy (both of these were later described as "histories"), or even synthetic compounds in which text and drawing are worked together into a kind of cryptogram (Fig. 2). In Northern France inventions of this sort often show an astonishing dexterity.

The official art of the Carolingians, which deliberately sought to recover the spirit of antique art, nearly everywhere suppressed these early efforts. But the Western instinct for decoration was only lulled asleep; freed by the disappearance of Carolingian art, it soon reawoke and gradually the Romanesque initial, heir to the precaroline, evolved. We shall see it grow in stature and complexity, embroidering on the antique themes of hunting and combat of which it was particularly fond, on motifs of both Christian and pagan inspiration, and on the rediscovered initials of Mero-

1 – MEROVINGIAN ZOOMORPHIC INITIAL. SACRAMENTARY OF GELLONE, SECOND HALF OF THE 8TH CENTURY (BIBLIOTHÈQUE NATIONALE, MS. LAT. 12048, F. 111 V.)

2 – INITIAL WITH FIGURES. CORBIE PSALTER, BEGINNING OF THE 9TH CENTURY (AMIENS, MS. 18, F. 67 V.)

vingian times, or finding in the text itself the themes for small narrative pictures. In the Romanesque period the Midi no less than the North cultivated the decorated initial, but composed it from different elements, knew nothing of the narrative "historiated" initial, and in general never combined the illustration of a text with its decoration. Therein lies one of the more striking differences between the two wings of the diptych.

The two wings do, however, have something in common, something that was, indeed, common to the whole of medieval art from its earliest period. Decorating a flat surface, the medieval artist scarcely tried to create an illusion of depth, whether by linear devices, by the use of shadows or by foreshortening. Sometimes, as we shall see, he did try to do so; and certain paintings, generally copies of antique or Byzantine models, reveal such a striking understanding of mass and proportion that we cannot but wonder how so gifted a copyist, so sure and brilliant a draughtsman, was not able, long before the first attempts of the 14th and 15th centuries, to work out for himself the rules of illusionism. But consciously or unconsciously his interest lay elsewhere. He was given a plane, and on this plane he projected his images, confining himself, when he wished to indicate the roundness of his forms, to certain more or less accurate indications of folds or colours. Indifferent to the outward look of the beings and objects surrounding us, he aspired to paint them as we know them to be, to grasp their essence in its entirety. The special perspective which he used was perfectly adapted to this end. Though different from ours it is no less true, if the observer, instead of being on a level with the picture, the horizon at the same height as his eye, looks down on it obliquely. From this angle the system of foreshortening seems to be reversed; it is as if the reader were sitting at a table, on which objects appear to him to be separate, distinct from one other and arranged in a vertical series.

It was only about the beginning of the 15th century, in a period which traditional chronology classifies as still medieval, that the vertical plane was tilted backwards, separating sky and landscape and concealing objects behind one another. Miniature painting, in its new-found concern for deep perspective, then began to approximate to panel painting. Adherence to the rule of the vertical plane has certain consequences. Perceived not as they appear to us, but as they really

3 – MASSACRE OF THE INNOCENTS. AUTUN TROPER, 996–1024 (BIBLIOTHÈQUE DE L'ARSENAL, MS. 1169, F. 15)

are, the important characters, human or divine—evangelists, authors, potentates—are portrayed in conformity with our idea of them, arranged in a material hierarchy not only by their place in the picture, which is self-evident, but by their stature or even by a deliberate distortion of their proportions. Buildings, on the other hand, and the various pieces of furniture are summarily indicated in two-dimensional silhouette and look as if pasted to the background. And yet the rule of the plane, like all rules, permits of subtle distinctions, and it is wrong to exaggerate its rigour. From the end of the 11th century onwards some painters, more alive than others to sensible appearances, attempted to portray depth, and we find these attempts specifically amongst those painters whose work was by now in large part or altogether unfettered by tradition—the painters of the Midi.

THE ORIGIN OF THE ROMANESQUE STYLE

FROM THE END OF THE 10TH CENTURY TO CIRCA 1130

Antique and Carolingian Survivals

Poor as the 10th century in France was by comparison with the imperial art of the Carolingians, a few miniatures have none the less survived from it. The technique of painting had been lost, but not the taste

for learning, which was kept alive in the great abbeys. Thanks to them the classical tradition inherited from the previous century left lasting traces.

The type of drawing found in 9th-century copies of Terence's comedies and of the poems of Prudentius illustrated after Late Antique models, notably at Fleury, recurs in a Troper from Autun dating from the time of King Robert and Bishop Gautier (996–1024; Fig. 3). It recurs again at Saint-Aubin, Angers, in the first half of the 11th century in a Terence and a *Lives of the Bishops of Angers* (Fig. 4). The district of the Loire long remained faithful to the traces of antique art which had inspired the famous centres of Saint-Martin at Tours and Marmoutiers; and this may perhaps explain why the illustrations in the early 11th-century manuscripts of the Abbey of Saint-Maur-des-Fossés near Paris, associated with that of Glanfeuil near Angers, present curious analogies with contem-

5 – SCENES FROM THE LIFE OF ST. MAURUS. LIVE AND MIRACLES OF ST. MAURUS, SECOND HALF OF THE 11TH CENTURY (TROYES, MS. 2273, F. 77)

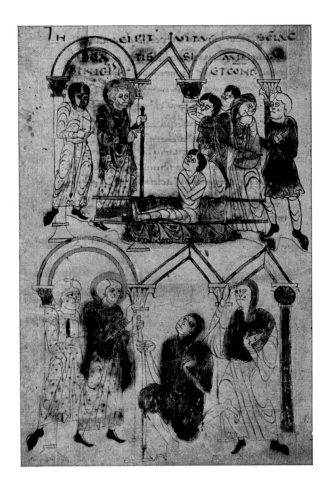

4 – SCENES FROM THE LIFE OF ST. ALBINUS. LIVES OF THE BISHOPS OF ANGERS, FIRST HALF OF THE 11TH CENTURY (VATICAN, MS. REGIN. LAT. 465, F. 74 V.)

porary drawings from Saint-Aubin. Its Missal and two copies of the *Life and Miracles of St. Maurus* (Fig. 5) are animated by stocky little figures, their draperies summarily indicated in line with no regard for the modelling of the muscles, like the characters in a Terence. Behind these figures runs a rudimentary architectural motif suggesting a building or a town. A *History of the foundation of Saint-Martin-des-Champs* (*circa* 1070) is in the same vein (Fig. 6).

It was the age of relics: sacred relics round which old abbeys were restored and new ones grew up. Many fresh copies were made of the *Lives* of saints, several of them illustrated; and nothing has a better claim to the name of popular art than the illumination of some of these *Lives*, youthful in the novelty of its subject matter and in its direct and spontaneous approach, but feeble in technique and backward in style. Such were the 10th-century *Lives of SS. Valericus and Philibert* and the *Life of St. Wandregisil* (Fig. 7) from Saint-Omer. Such too was the later *Life of St. Quintinus*. The agreeable roughness of these simple, unpretentious paintings and their lively charm should not deceive us. Whatever their origin, they simply reassemble old elements or copy Carolingian paintings (perhaps frescoes), and they are the sign not of a rebirth but of a death, the death of the antique forms that had nurtured the rising art of the West. A comparison between the scenes in a manuscript of Prudentius

and those in the *Life of St. Wandregisil* affords eloquent proof of this assertion, if due allowance is made for the intervention, even at this early stage, of factors which disrupt the methodical tidiness of our categories.

Such links with the Mediterranean world, ancient and contemporary alike, had been traditional since Carolingian times and their influence was still apparent in a variety of ways. A copy of the Gospels made at about the end of the 10th century, perhaps in some Angevin abbey, contains a much altered inscription which indicates that its archetype derived from the bookseller Gaudiosus, who kept a shop near the church of St. Peter ad Vincula in Rome, perhaps in the 8th century. At Fleury, early in the 11th century, Abbot Gauzelin commissioned the Lombard artist Nivardus to decorate a magnificent Gospel-lectionary in gold and silver letters on purple parchment, a fact

which says much for the artistic poverty of his otherwise important abbey. At Montmajour a handsome Lectionary, also of the 11th century, again reveals the proximity of Lombard Italy in the drawing of the closely-woven pointed interlace of its decorated initials and in the amplitude of its figures (Isaiah, St. Paul praying before Christ); as does also, less obviously, a Gospel-book from Aix (Fig. 8).

There was nothing coherent or organic about these developments. Borrowings from the past and chance contacts hold no promise for the future, for that requires a more powerful impulse, the dominating influence of a living art. In the North of France just such an influence was brought to bear in the course of the 11th century by two centres in particular—England and the district of the Meuse and Rhine. In the Midi, directly or indirectly, the dominating influence was Byzantium. Of course, these contemporary in-

6 – FOUNDATION OF SAINT-MARTIN-DES-CHAMPS. HISTORY OF SAINT-MARTIN-DES-CHAMPS, CIRCA 1067–1079 (BRITISH MUSEUM, ADD. MS. 11662, F. 4)

7 – SCENES FROM THE LIFE OF ST. WANDREGISIL. LIVE OF ST. WANDREGISIL, 10TH CENTURY (SAINT-OMER, MS. 764, F. 9)

qd hoc compati oportuerit & ut illic esse donec meos uenirec · uir aines
amonuit · sic benedix eos & recessit · reliquidqᵍ laudares dm · in templo · ꝑ̄c̄ ·

8 – ST. LUKE. GOSPEL BOOK, SECOND HALF OF THE 11TH CENTURY
(AIX-EN-PROVENCE, MS. 7, F. 169)

fluences did not entirely efface the Carolingian and
even antique traditions on to which they were
grafted. French Romanesque painting was the product of a variety of influences, ancient and contemporary alike, and it was to blend them together, and
little by little to emancipate itself from them; although
full emancipation came only at the end of the Romanesque period.

Carolingian survivals were everywhere to be found,
but they were cherished with particular devotion at
Saint-Martial, Limoges, down to the end of the 10th
century. They include scrolls, palmettes, foliage and
boldly-drawn animals, as found at Saint-Martin,
Tours, in the time of Alcuin (796–804). A Lectionary from the same abbey adds to this Carolingian
repertoire not only zoomorphic initials from an even

earlier Merovingian source, but copies of contemporary Byzantine ivories which had doubtless reached
there by way of Germany (Pl. 1 and Fig. 9). Situated
on the border between the North and the Midi, the
great abbey at Limoges soon turned its attention
to Aquitaine; but at this early date Aquitaine had as
yet no art of its own (see p. 25).

Other obvious Carolingian survivals are to be found
at Paris nearly a century later. What Saint-Martial

9 – ST. PETER. IVORY. COVER OF THE GRADUAL OF HENRY II,
CIRCA 1000 (BAMBERG, STAATSBIBLIOTHEK, MS. LIT. 7)

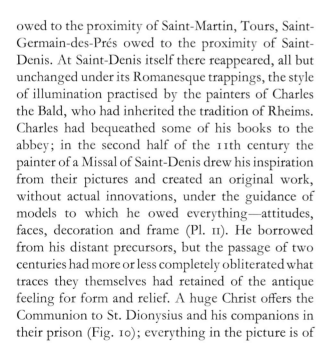

10 — COMMUNION OF ST. DIONYSIUS. MISSAL OF SAINT-DENIS, MIDDLE OF THE 11TH CENTURY (BIBLIOTHÈQUE NATIONALE, MS. LAT. 9436, F. 106 V.)

11 — ST. MARK. GOSPEL BOOK OF SAINT-VANNE, FIRST HALF OF THE 12TH CENTURY (VERDUN, MS. 43, F. 28 V.)

owed to the proximity of Saint-Martin, Tours, Saint-Germain-des-Prés owed to the proximity of Saint-Denis. At Saint-Denis itself there reappeared, all but unchanged under its Romanesque trappings, the style of illumination practised by the painters of Charles the Bald, who had inherited the tradition of Rheims. Charles had bequeathed some of his books to the abbey; in the second half of the 11th century the painter of a Missal of Saint-Denis drew his inspiration from their pictures and created an original work, without actual innovations, under the guidance of models to which he owed everything—attitudes, faces, decoration and frame (Pl. 11). He borrowed from his distant precursors, but the passage of two centuries had more or less completely obliterated what traces they themselves had retained of the antique feeling for form and relief. A huge Christ offers the Communion to St. Dionysius and his companions in their prison (Fig. 10); everything in the picture is of

Carolingian origin, except the exaggerated height of Our Lord, which conforms to the Romanesque canon. And yet the hard, abrupt modelling, emphasized by black lines, flattens contours instead of rounding them, and the crenellated wall which in Carolingian painting represented an earthly or heavenly city is here transformed, towards the back of the picture, into a jagged rainbow which is purely decorative and flies in the face of logic.

Not far from Saint-Denis, at Saint-Germain-des-Prés, under Abbot Adelard (*circa* 1030–1060), the scribe and painter Ingelard decorated a Lectionary and a Psalter (Pl. 111) whose delicately tinted drawings against green and violet backgrounds also derive from the Carolingian style of Rheims, but, this time, from the Rheims style of Hautvillers and Archbishop Ebbo (*circa* 830). Can we speak of a Parisian school? Saint-Denis and Saint-Germain-des-Prés followed Rheims; Saint-Maur followed Angers. The manner

15

12 – CHRIST BETWEEN SS. BENEDICT AND GREGORY. HOMILIES ON EZECHIEL, 10TH CENTURY (ORLÉANS, MS. 175, P. 150)

in which French Romanesque developed is here plainly revealed: the receptivity of artists quick to take their chances, to seize whatever came to hand since they lacked a tradition of their own, and to dress it up after their own fashion since they were unfettered by any formula. Ingelard's Lectionary gives pride of place to the life of St. Dionysius, and there may well be a good reason for this: the Parisian painters went to school among the books of his famous abbey. Similar Carolingian survivals may lie behind the handsome Lectionary of Saint-André, at Le Cateau (Pl. IV). It is far superior to the work that was being done a few years earlier, in the middle of the 11th century, at the neighbouring Abbey of Saint-Sépulcre, at Cambrai, including a *Moralia* of St. Gregory which is in the same style as the *Lives* of saints referred to above.

An even more surprising, because later, example of such mimicry is an early 12th-century Gospel-book from the Abbey of Saint-Vanne, Verdun. With portraits of the Evangelists copied from a Rheims model, it combines Franco-Saxon canon tables: two quite distinct Carolingian types deliberately chosen and reproduced with scrupulous care (Fig. 11).

The English Contribution

Of the abbeys bordering on the Loire the most venerable was Fleury, which preserved the link with the Carolingian era, and which, as we have already observed, had a taste for drawings in imitation of the antique style. Beginning in the 10th century, continuous contact with England, for which there is documentary evidence, was to make itself felt in its manuscripts. A copy of St. Gregory's *Homilies on Ezechiel*, which a dedicatory inscription in green and red capital letters shows to have been written at Fleury, and which is decorated with initials clearly painted at the abbey, contains a large drawing, certainly by an English hand, of Christ in a mandorla between SS. Gregory and Benedict (Fig. 12). Abbo, who was Abbot of Fleury from 988 to 1004, had spent two years at Ramsey Abbey and had brought back presents, including manuscripts. His successor Gauzelin, who commissioned the Gospel-book from Nivardus, was to receive books from Ramsey and Winchcombe.

Odbert, Abbot of Saint-Bertin from 986 to 1004, was acquainted with certain aspects of Carolingian art;

13 – NATIVITY AND ANNUNCIATION TO THE SHEPHERDS. PSALTER OF ODBERT, CIRCA 1000 (BOULOGNE, MS. 20, F. 58 V.)

but he was himself a painter—he signed his most beautiful work, a Psalter (Fig. 13)—and he interpreted them in his own way. He owed this interpretation to his English neighbours. If the marginal figures in his Psalter, which may be the work of collaborators under his direction, recall the figures of the former school of Rheims (those in the Gospel-book of Archbishop Ebbo, *circa* 825–830, and in the so-called Utrecht Psalter), it is because his English masters were entirely dependent on the Rheims style, and it was from England that he took both his style and his technique. Not only did he imitate English artists, he brought several to work in his monastery; and one of them decorated a superb Gospel-lectionary written at Saint-Bertin in his time (Pl. v). But although Odbert put himself to school under English masters, he did not follow them slavishly, for he knew how to take ideas from other sources and blend them with theirs. He was familiar with the work of the earliest Saint-Bertin artists, in the reign of Louis the Pious, deriving from it the volutes in his corner-pieces and the fillets in his frames. Apart from his Psalter, we possess several Gospel-books from his hand (one contains a Christ in Majesty copied from an English painter and so proves his English connections); a copy of the *Phaenomena* of Aratus in which the figures of the constellations reproduce those of a Carolingian manuscript now at Leyden, itself imitating an antique

14 – DAVID AND THE SHULAMITE: APPEARANCE OF THE LORD TO
SOLOMON. BIBLE OF SAINT-VAAST, FIRST HALF OF THE 11TH
CENTURY (ARRAS, MS. 435, VOL. I, F. 128 V.)

fied his staple English diet in many ways. His greedy
eclecticism and unbridled curiosity are typical of the
early Romanesque period in general, and yet his personality was strong enough, even then, to stamp his
faces with features that were all his own (true, they are
all alike). He created a style and imparted it to his collaborators, since the decoration of his manuscripts is
obviously not all by his own hand. His taste for
colour was reliable, as may be seen in a Martyrdom of
St. Dionysius (Pl. VII) painted in a harmony of pink
and silver.

Soon after the time of Odbert at Saint-Bertin, the
Abbey of Saint-Vaast, Arras, started work on a Bible
in four large volumes. It appears that the scribes, at
least six in number, were also the decorators (Fig 14).
The monks of Saint-Vaast began by following English
art even more closely than the monks of Saint-Bertin;
but whereas Odbert had directed the artistic activity
of his abbey and was himself an artist, the Arras
group seem to have formed a kind of artistic co-oper-
ative, without strong direction. Their Bible, which
is the masterpiece of painting at Arras, suffers from
the want of it. It is a strange and beautiful work,
astonishingly composite, in which as at Saint-Bertin
the most disparate influences meet but never blend,
in pictures which are often badly composed and sometimes positively clumsy. But it appeals to us through
its very defects, which expose the elements of which
it is made. It was appallingly mutilated in the 19th
century, but incomplete and half-ruined though it is,
the Bible deserves to be closely studied, since it testi-
fies to a commendable, even bold enterprise. These
men who set out to give their abbey a book worthy of
its name followed the best available models, namely
the English successors to the artists of the Bene-
dictional of St. Aethelwold; they strove to imitate
their style of drawing, and we see in the Bible a
ponderous version of their lively and nervous line.
Their decoration is the so-called Winchester decoration, but thinner and more linear, with heavy rosettes
in the corners and uprights of the frames. That was
not all: in their search for precedents they turned to
the famous works of past and more glorious ages,
and some of their miniatures can only be explained
by supposing that they knew the illustrations of a
manuscript similar to the Lorsch Gospels, or the
Gospels of Saint-Médard, Soissons. Thus it was the
Carolingians and the English who fostered the art of
Saint-Vaast, as they had the art of Saint-Bertin.

model; and, a more original work, a *Lives of SS. Bertinus, Folquinus, Silvinus and Winnoc,* which is a compen-
dium of easily recognisable borrowings. St. Bertinus
and his companions, for example, appear in a frame
in the Carolingian Franco-Saxon style as revised in
England; it is surmounted by a profusion of architectural motifs also drawn from the Carolingian repertoire but enriched by Ottonian features of the kind
found at Cologne, and embellished with palmettes,
which in spite of their greater stylization recall the
manuscripts of Charles the Bald, and with medallions
decorated with strange Anglo-Irish beasts (Pl. VI).
Odbert took something from everywhere and diversi-

15 – ST. AUGUSTINE. ST. AUGUSTINE, DE CIVITATE DEI, END OF
THE 11TH CENTURY (BIBLIOTHÈQUE NATIONALE, MS. LAT. 2058,
F. 1)

There existed at Saint-Vaast, contemporary with the Bible and grouped around it, a number of manuscripts in which we can descry another influence, absent at Saint-Bertin, that of antique art: as clearly in direct borrowings—caryatids, personifications of the winds, sphinxes, or the angel in a copy of St. Gregory—as in the partly marginal illustrations to a Gospel-lectionary, now at Boulogne, in which, oddly enough, we find ideas closely resembling Odbert's and, in places, the same style. We know the names of many of the Saint-Vaast scribes, who were without doubt painters as well, since the style of certain paintings corresponds with certain handwritings. Alardus copied a *Confessions* of St. Augustine (Pl. VIII), and if he painted the miniature on its opening leaf, he also painted the leaf with large figures in the first volume of the Bible. If Albertus decorated with his own hand the *Miracles of St. Vedastus* which he signed, he also painted at least three illustrations in the second and third volumes of the Bible. The names of the other painters of the Bible are unknown, but they may well be hidden among the names of the scribes given at the beginning and end of each gathering of a copy of the *Disciplina Ecclesiastica* of Regino of Prüm, which was the work of at least ten monks, among them the

Albertus and Alardus mentioned above. The workshop that produced the Saint-Vaast Bible is, therefore, well known to us; we can even see it at work, depicted in the liveliest possible fashion, on the first page of the Bible.

Fleury, Saint-Bertin and Saint-Vaast all introduced English art and artists on a large scale, but their enterprises were local ones and in general had no lasting effect: the work of individuals, as at Fleury and Saint-Bertin, or of a group, as at Saint-Vaast, they hardly survived their authors. Nothing shows more clearly how empty is the conception of school or workshop when applied to French Romanesque painting, at least in its early stages. Useful enough as a means of arranging paintings in place or time, it may none the less falsify our perspective and lead us to attribute a degree of continuity to what in fact were isolated achievements as ephemeral as the men who inspired them, to be followed, sometimes after a long interval, sometimes not at all, by fresh achievements of a totally different kind.

In the history of artistic contacts between France and England Normandy is a special case. After the Norman conquest the two shores of the Channel formed a single unit which historians find it difficult to divide and the question is further complicated by the fact that the creation of the Anglo-Norman kingdom gave a new character to the decoration of manuscripts in its territories. In England the art of illumination changed, or at least was modified; in Normandy, more strikingly, it was created. At first sight it looks as if the determining influence was that of England on Normandy, but at closer range the matter is not so simple. The two most important works of art with figures that we come across in Normandy immediately after the conquest are English. For the Bayeux Tapestry, convincing proof of this has recently been adduced; it seems certain that it was commissioned from English embroiderers between 1077 and 1082 by Odo, Bishop of Bayeux, to mark the dedication of his cathedral. Again, in 1082, when the Conqueror's brother Robert founded a collegiate church at Mortain in honour of St. Ebrulf, his gifts included a Gospel-book, the decoration of which he commissioned from an English painter. On the other hand, from the end of the 11th century onwards, there is nothing to connect with England either the series of manuscripts executed at Mont-Saint-Michel or the distinct group executed in Lower

Normandy. Apart from an early 11th-century copy of the *Recognitiones* of St. Clement that begins with an interesting but rough painting of the scribe presenting his book to St. Michael (Pl. IX), and a later Sacramentary (end of the century) of similar inspiration to a *Civitas Dei* from Canterbury, now in Florence, which is certainly by an English hand, the manuscripts of Mont-Saint-Michel form a homogeneous group. Their contents are all patristic (SS. Augustine, Ambrose, Jerome) and the text is generally preceded by a large portrait of the author writing or disputing, painted in dull colours dominated by chalky greens and pinks. They are quite independent of English art and seem to have been influenced by the neighbouring province of Anjou (Pl. x). The great family of Lower Norman abbeys, Bayeux, Saint-Évroult, Lyre, Préaulx, La-Croix-Saint-Leufroi, Le Bec, are again remarkably uniform in style, favouring initial letters with heavily modelled foliage, preferably in red and green, embellished with human figures and dragons and various kinds of animal (Pl. XI and Fig. 15). There is no denying that this style produced a change of taste in England. We know that William of Saint-Calais, Bishop of Durham, returned from his exile in Normandy (1088–1091) with a number of books which served as models for his own decorators. The thesis that the Normans imparted certain ideas to their English neighbours, but that the debt contracted by the latter was simply the result of taking

17 – NEBUCHADNEZOR AND THE JEWS IN THE FURNACE. BIBLE OF STEPHEN HARDING, BEGINNING OF THE 12TH CENTURY (DIJON, MS. 14, F. 64)

16 – DECORATED INITIAL. ST. GREGORY, MORALIA IN JOB, BEGINNING OF THE 12TH CENTURY (DIJON, MS. 170, F. 59)

back some of what they had themselves previously lent, has been argued tenaciously and is perfectly possible. Similar processes may as easily be shown to have taken place almost anywhere. It is better, however, to keep to general outlines, lest one complicate still further a question already all too confused by uncertainties of date and place. What was the origin of this artistic tendency in the abbeys of Lower Normandy? Burgundy, perhaps, if the same tendency appears at about this time at Cîteaux, in a collection of the *Letters* of St. Jerome: a simple hypothesis that I will not insist upon in view of what I have just said. We ought, however, to bear in mind the relations established in the course of the 11th century by William of Volpiano and by Suppo, Abbot of Mont-Saint-Michel, between Saint-Bénigne, Dijon, and Lower Normandy. Personal contacts may well have forged artistic links of the kind clearly established between Normandy and England by Lanfranc and St.

Anselm, who were successively monks at Avranches and Le Bec and Archbishops of Canterbury. But in fact the comparison delays without answering the question: what is the origin of Burgundian decoration? We must resign ourselves to not knowing all the answers and to finding ourselves confronted with artists who are inventive enough to confuse the scent. As French painters establish their independence, this same situation will constantly repeat itself, and the hunt for artistic influences, acceptable enough as a means of clarifying origins, will more than once be frustrated by an original talent which makes a mockery of our categories and which we must learn not to question but simply to accept.

In Burgundy itself, at Cîteaux, at the beginning of the eleventh century, there appeared two styles, unrelated to one another and utterly different in technique and in inspiration, even though they are separated at most by only a few years: a belated but perfect example of the coexistence at one place of differing, even rival "schools". The style of the first group looks to England (which is why it belongs here). Unless the connection is direct and the group no more than a single artist; for there is nothing to show that Stephen Harding, the monk of Sherborne who in 1109 became Abbot of Cîteaux and ruled the abbey until 1133, was not the sole author of the witty drawings, touched with washes, that illustrate a Bible in four volumes which he himself revised for the use of his monks. The first two volumes were finished, as far as the scribes' work was concerned, in 1109, the year in which Stephen became Abbot. The others, in a different format, were written after his arrival and more richly decorated, with initials peopled by characters whose lively good humour, tinged with irony, has no parallel in France at that period. These characters come from the Abbot's own entourage and are drawn from life (perhaps a unique case) in a spirit of gentle caricature (Fig. 16). The same spirit recurs in a copy of St. Gregory's *Moralia* in four volumes, three of which had been completed by 24th December, 1111. These tinted drawings have nothing in common with contemporary French art; on the contrary, everything connects them with the English tradition: vivacity of line, sense of humour (already), and their light colouring. If they are not the work of Harding, they were executed by some other Englishman, also from Sherborne or thereabouts. Besides the initials, the two books contain large paintings which reveal a

18 – THE CREATION. COMMENTARIES ON THE BIBLE; VENDÔME, FIRST HALF OF THE 12TH CENTURY (VENDÔME, MS. 117, F. 1)

masterly talent for decoration, among them an initial *R* formed of two superimposed figures, elegant athletes attacking a dragon (Pl. XII). The narrative scenes, like those of the life of David, are clear and well-arranged despite the crowd of little figures cramped together in several registers. At the beginning of the Book of Daniel is a fat and furious Nebuchadnezor, thoroughly comic, whom a courtier can barely restrain from throwing himself upon the three men whom the Lord is protecting from the fire (Fig. 17). Harding appears here in an unexpected

light. Even if we admit that he was not himself the artist of the pictures in his Bible, they were painted under his supervision and their generous, tonic art shows that this man whom the written sources describe as a pillar of the strict and even harsh Cistercian observance, this scrupulous corrector of the Scriptures, was also a lover of gaiety and an observant man who delighted in his surroundings and knew how to draw from familiar scenes a composition that was at once highly decorative and full of freedom. Thus does the evidence of works of art complete and enrich the evidence of written history.

We have reached the beginning of the 12th century, when for the time being the influence of the British Isles was interrupted. Harding was in this respect already isolated, a *retardataire*. But before passing on to another phase in the French apprenticeship, we must notice a curious case of imitation of English art at La Trinité, Vendôme. The introductory miniature in a Commentary on the first four books of the Bible dating from the first half of the 12th century and written, if not at Vendôme itself, at least in France, recalls in a general way the Harrowing of Hell in an English Psalter of *circa* 1050. It portrays the Creation (Fig. 18). Attended by three angels with crossed wings God the Father, with a cruciform nimbus like Christ's in the Harrowing of Hell, bends forward over Chaos and disengages the sky and its stars, the sea and its fish and the earth, represented by stylized plants towards which four animals are leaping. A new wave of English influence was to be felt during the last few years of the century, but the welcome accorded to it by the French was to be very different. Full of new strength, on the threshold of the Gothic age in which their mastery was to be confirmed, they knew how to learn from it instead of merely copying it; and the foreign and the native streams were intimately commingled.

The German Contribution

Just as the North-West turned towards England, so the East of France was bound to turn towards its Ottonian neighbour, towards the art of the German kingdom. At the beginning of the 11th century Abbot Suthard of Saint-Pierre, Senones, near Saint-Dié, commissioned a Gospel-book whose initials contain a kind of interlace found only in the region between the Rhine and the Moselle, at the Abbey of Echter-

19 – MIRACLES OF ST. MARTIN. COLLECTANEA ON ST. MARTIN, FIRST HALF OF THE 12TH CENTURY (ÉPINAL, MS. 73, F. 5 V.)

nach for instance: broad, tightly-woven, flowering out here and there into round or globular petals, and drawn in red on a background of bare parchment. Its Canon Tables, on the other hand, are in the Franco-Saxon style, with the curious beast's head in which that style delighted and which Anglo-Irish decorators had derived from the Middle East or beyond. We have already noticed this Carolingian survival on the banks of the Meuse (p. 17). Another Gospel-book from Lorraine—its exact origin is unknown, but it

20 – PENTECOST. LECTIONARY FROM CLUNY, END OF THE 11TH
CENTURY (BIBLIOTHÈQUE NATIONALE, MS. NOUV. ACQ. LAT.
2246, F. 79 V.)

21 – THE BAPTISM OF CHRIST; THE MARRIAGE AT CANA. SACRA-
MENTARY OF SAINT-ÉTIENNE; LIMOGES, CIRCA 1100 (BIBLIO-
THÈQUE NATIONALE, MS. LAT. 9438, F. 24)

belongs a little earlier, at the end of the 10th century
—contains gold initials ringed with red in the form
of branches, which recall certain paintings from Saint-
Gall. But the most active centre in Lorraine about
the year 1100 was the Abbey of Saint-Vanne in the
Diocese of Verdun, which Abbot Richard had at
the beginning of the 11th century made the centre of
a monastic reform that embraced a number of com-
munities in the district of the Meuse. The Gospel-

books and Lectionaries decorated for his abbey, with
initials containing figures drawn in outline and sober-
ly tinted with blue, violet, green and red, recall by
their classical elegance the paintings executed towards
the end of the 10th century for Egbert, Archbishop
of Trier, by the great artist who is known as the
Master of the *Registrum Gregorii*, after a manuscript
of his now in the library at Trier. At Metz, at the
Abbey of Saint-Martin, at much the same time, two

22 – BISHOP LEANDER; AQUITAINIAN INITIAL. ST. GREGORY, MORALIA IN JOB, END OF THE 11TH CENTURY (BORDEAUX, MS. 24, F. 1)

church in Christendom) exhibit an obvious and close relationship with Ottonian art; and documentary evidence, too often wanting for other centres, supports the evidence of the paintings. Abbot Hugo (1049–1109) had not only spread the glory and influence of Cluny throughout the whole of Europe; a godfather of Henry IV of Germany, he was at Canossa when on 28th January, 1077, Gregory VII agreed to receive the Emperor and, at his instance and that of Countess Matilda of Tuscany, to pardon him; and as counsellor to that Pope and to his successor Urban II, whose master he had been at Cluny, he never ceased to intercede for his godson. His persevering friendship for this descendant of the Ottos may perhaps explain why painting at Cluny was inspired by the best model of the period, namely Ottonian art, and through it by the art of Byzantium, from which the Ottonian artists had borrowed so much. We have nothing but ruins to judge by, among others a mutilated Lectionary of the end of the 11th century, saved from the savage destruction which befell everything that came from Cluny. It contains no more than six paintings, with initials in the Rhenish style (Fig. 20). Oddly enough, the technique of these paintings appears Byzantine in its fragility; so much so that we are entitled to wonder whether some foreign master was not working at Cluny at the time.

The part played by Ottonian art in the formation of French art may be seen, even more distinctly, in a Sacramentary from the Cathedral of Saint-Étienne, Limoges, of the late 11th or early 12th century. The vigour of the drawing, its schematic character, and certain details of the decoration, associate this strange and magnificent work with the general characteristics of Limoges illumination, and even with the South; but the overall effect is infinitely more complex, severe and even hard. The colouring is hot and violent, the modelling abrupt. The figures, with their slender, sinewy forms and the pathos of their attitudes, suggest an Ottonian model of the 11th century, reworked and dramatized by a Limoges artist; but the exact origin of the model remains to be discovered. This connection is also indicated by certain details of iconography. The Jordan is represented by two river-gods, Jor and Dan, as in a Gradual from the Abbey of Prüm, in the Rhineland (Fig. 21). The Ascension is of a type which was not then known in France but which occurs in a Gospel-lectionary from

drawings tinted with bright yellow illustrate a collection of texts on St. Martin which is a replica of a volume now at Trier (Pl. XIII and Fig. 19).

At this early stage Romanesque contacts with Germany were not confined to the North-East of France. What remain of the manuscripts of Cluny (they were dispersed in 1809–1813 at the time of the demolition of this the largest and most beautiful monastic

Salzburg (Pl. XIV). The waving ribbons which unite Christ in the Pentecost with his disciples derive from the inverted, more or less stylized torches, which at Reichenau and Ratisbon were regularly used as symbols of heavenly or prophetic inspiration. Lastly, the *clavi*, gold rectangles freely used to decorate garments, were otherwise unknown in France and so certainly come from models such as the Gospel-lectionary of Bamberg Cathedral, of the beginning of the 9th century. It has also been observed that in drawing and colouring the paintings in the Sacramentary closely resemble Limoges enamels. Who knows whether the technique of enamelling, which afterwards achieved such splendours at Limoges, may not have had as its point of departure Ottonian en-

24 – ST. MICHAEL. ST. JOHN CHRYSOSTOM, HOMILIES, CIRCA 1078 (BIBLIOTHÈQUE NATIONALE, MS. COISL. 79, F. 2 V.)

amel-work, which had been so brilliant in previous centuries and which was itself the descendant of Byzantine enamelling? The great Bible of the collegiate church at Saint-Yrieix, to-day in the town-hall, is contemporary with the Sacramentary of Saint-Étienne, whose style and colouring it in part resembles. Both works must belong to the same pictorial tradition.

The Mediterranean Contribution

The first traces of French art in the South appear about the year 1000 in the district round Albi. Interlace, a simple pattern inherited from pre-Roman times and diffused throughout Europe, has in Languedoc and the adjacent provinces a particular thread-like form. It is generally "reserved" against a ground of dark colour—purple, green, deep violet—and ends in broad branches or palmettes with flat spear-shaped leaves. These palmettes derive from Byzantine capi-

23 – DECORATED INITIAL. BIBLE OF THE GRANDE-CHARTREUSE, BEGINNING OF THE 12TH CENTURY (GRENOBLE, MS. 17, F. 175)

25 – CANON TABLES. BIBLE OF SAINT-MARTIAL; LIMOGES, SECOND HALF OF THE 10TH CENTURY (BIBLIOTHÈQUE NATIONALE, MS. LAT. 5, VOL. II, F. 131)

26 – CANON TABLES. GOSPEL BOOK, END OF THE 11TH CENTURY (PERPIGNAN, MS. I, F. 13 V.)

tals of the period of Justinian (527–565), as found at Hagia Sophia in Constantinople or at S. Vitale at Ravenna, to name two examples. Their style has been called "colourist". The derivation is all the more obvious because the painter, in order to detach his pattern from its background, employed colour to reproduce the sharp effect of high relief, in which the pattern looks white against the black shadows in the areas where the stone has been cut away (Pl. xv). "Reserved" interlace occurs elsewhere—in Germany (we have already seen examples of it there), in Italy and in Spain, and before that in the decoration of Insular manuscripts; but nowhere else is it accompanied by palmettes of this sort. Round Narbonne the palmette is somewhat different: still flat, but

broad, jagged and striated (Fig. 22). This sort comes from Monte Cassino (how and why we shall see in a moment); and it may have inspired the artist who in about 1100 decorated the curious Bibles of the Grande-Chartreuse (Fig. 23). At Albi itself the gold filigree work in a Psalter (Pl. XVII) can best be compared with similar work that borders the robes of St. Michael and the Emperor Nicephorus Botaniates (1078-1081) in a famous copy of the works of St. John Chrysostom of which he himself was the owner (Fig. 24). These modest but undeniable indications, the Aquitanian palmette and the filigree work, reveal the distant origins, direct or indirect, of Romanesque art in the Midi: the eastern Mediterranean and Byzantium.

Another sign of this connection—we shall see several —a sign no less eloquent of Byzantium although not so exclusively confined to Languedoc, are the scenes of fighting monsters crowded onto the vertical faces of pilasters and "reserved" against a coloured background, an example of the influence of sculpture. The later development of this decorative theme is well known. It appears in sculpture at Moissac from the end of the 11th century onwards, but it is also to be found two hundred years earlier at Tours, in Carolingian manuscripts of the time of Alcuin, and in the 10th century, doubtless derived from Tours, at Saint-Martial, Limoges (Fig. 25). This Tours formula was also drawn from the Greek East (perhaps *via* Britain, but that is another story). It reaches its climax at Roussillon (Fig. 26). Fighting animals and hunting-scenes occur in profusion in Byzantine ivories, diptychs, caskets, horns, and in Roman mosaics; and if the destruction of medieval works of art in the Near East had been less disastrous, we should doubtless possess more stone reliefs like the fragment now in the Louvre, coming from Athens, yet already so close to Languedoc in style that it would not be out of place at Moissac (Fig. 27). By what routes the palmette and the fighting animals infiltrated into the Midi at this period we do not exactly know, but as much as of Constantinople or Ravenna or Monte Cassino, we must think of Spain. Mozarabic art owes much to the Eastern Mediterranean, and it may have been through Spain that the vital influence of Byzantium reached Southern France.

The famous copy of the Commentary on the Apocalypse composed by Beatus, a monk of Liebana, illuminated in the 11th century at the Abbey of Saint-Sever in Gascony, is a gallicised replica of the Mozarabic manuscripts of Beatus: gallicised, but none the less preserving many traces of its origin—the rich and brilliant colours, the animated and sprightly figures, and above all certain precise details of the decoration. Here everything is opposed to the art of the North. The drawing is simple and bold. The rigorously unbroken colours are dominated by a lively red and a bright yellow that are thoroughly Castilian. The figures are intensely alive and their demeanour is full of fire, in spite of the absence of relief (Pl. XVIII). The name Stephanus Garsia, which occurs in the volume, may be that of the painter who illuminated the book during the abbacy of Gregory Muntaner (1028–1072). Garsia was a common enough name in

Gascony in those days and need not mean that the artist was a Spaniard. He interpreted his model like the impetuous decorator that he was, so as to give the greatest possible pleasure to the eye. From the Spanish Beatus manuscripts he drew a few pages which are worthy of a place among the marvels of Romanesque painting in the West and which owe nothing, either in technique or in inspiration, to the great contemporary schools of England and the Rhineland. The

27 – FIGHTING ANIMALS. MARBLE, GREECE, 11TH CENTURY (PARIS, MUSÉE DU LOUVRE)

28 – APOSTLE. MARBLE, TOULOUSE, END OF THE 11TH CENTURY (TOULOUSE, ÉGLISE SAINT-SERNIN)

South, centred on the Mediterranean, enriched in art as in literature by contact with a civilisation which was able to transmit, in however changed a form, recollections of the antique world and of the East, entered the Romanesque era with a masterpiece which surpassed anything that the North, in spite of its greater diversity and prolificacy, had so far produced. It is wild and grandiose, and a Commentary on the Apocalypse is a fitting subject for this tumultuous revelation of southern painting.

But the Romanesque Midi has another more amiable side, which is apparent in other paintings contemporary with the Saint-Sever manuscript and coming like it from the region of Auch. There are, for instance, standing out in the same bold silhouette and dazzling our eyes with the same colours as Garcia's monsters, the dancing women and jugglers in a Troper familiar to musicologists: a collection of chants designed to accompany the Office, which they develop and paraphrase, but whose illustrations contain no liturgical allusions and might just as well decorate the verses of some troubadour (Pl. XVI).

These were promising beginnings, but here as elsewhere in French Romanesque painting they did not last long and had no posterity. No tradition was created in the country round Auch, and once the men who like Abbot Muntaner and others had been patrons of the Gascon artists had disappeared, the art of Saint-Sever disappeared likewise. Almost immediately, Southern painting was born again not far away at Toulouse, at the same moment as the art of sculpture, neglected in France since the Gallo-Roman period. The rude and fleshy figures which serve as frontispiece to a late 11th-century copy of the *De Bello Judaico* of Flavius Josephus gaily betoken this revival. Their unbroken colours relate them to the jugglers of the Troper but are more discreet, as if muted. The volume reached Paris in the 17th century among a group of manuscripts from Moissac, but its place of origin was somewhere in the vicinity of Saint-Sernin, Toulouse (Pl. XIX). On a double page, Titus and Vespasian sit grandly on their thrones, the imperial insignia in their hands and crowns on their heads, while Josephus, running forward along a road paved in the Roman fashion, presents, laid out on a cloth, the book that he has dedicated to them. Behind Josephus the crowd, simply drawn in outline, presses forward, curious—an inscription tells us—to discover for themselves what is in the book. All is life and movement, in spite of the artist's limited technique and his flippancy or clumsiness (he has deprived Josephus of his left arm). Though working flatly on a two-dimensional surface, he none the less has a feeling for depth and renders it in his own way, which is ingenious enough. A vertical band cuts off the figures of the crowd and they are slightly displaced in an upward direction so as to push them into the background; but some of their legs overlap the imaginary proscenium arch, and thanks to this simple device the

29 – HEAD OF AN ANGEL. FRESCO, SANT'ANGELO IN FORMIS, END OF THE 11TH CENTURY

low foreheads, the great eyes blazing out from plump faces, the hooked noses, the round bellies tightly swathed in metallic draperies, the stick-like legs—all these details betray their common descent (Fig. 28). Here again Byzantium comes to the surface. The draperies with their concentric folds and the type of face reproduce in detail the attitudes and the faces—low foreheads, huge black eyes, hooked noses between full cheeks—of, to take one example, the angels at Sant' Angelo in Formis, near Capua, which were painted in the time of Abbot Desiderius of Monte Cassino (1058–1086) and derive directly from Byzantium (Fig. 29; see also Fig. 24). And if they were not the actual models, others exactly like them were soon brought to Roussillon—though not, it is true, without damage in transit, as may be seen in the frescoes of Saint-Martin, Fenollar. But there is no trace here of anything Spanish. Are we then to suppose some personal contact between Toulouse and Monte Cassino? Direct contact certainly existed between Aragon and the Holy See, since the famous Gregory VII, who preceded Desiderius (Victor III) as Pope, was accepted as overlord in 1068 by King Sancho Ramirez (1063–1094) and kept a permanent legate at his court. The same situation was to be repeated a few years later in Catalonia; and the relations maintained between the Pope and Raymond IV, Count of Saint-Gilles, who was to succeed his brother William in the County of Toulouse in 1088, were hardly less close. Faced by the Mohammedan threat, the Papacy was

figures seem to spring out from the page. As at Saint-Sever, the figures are beings without volume, mere shadows, waiting to fill out and come to life. The realism of the Midi, by a strange detour, has travelled back to join hands with antique illusionism.

We shall observe elsewhere certain isolated signs of the same confused aspiration towards a return to the portrayal of sensible appearances, but they are nowhere so clear as at Toulouse. The taste for solid, tangible matter, scarcely expressed in painting for want of a suitable technique, can be seen in the sculpture of Saint-Sernin, where the use of relief makes possible a literal representation of volume and depth. Whatever the origin of sculpture in Languedoc (it is still a subject of controversy), the painting is derived from it. Airy and weightless, Josephus, Titus and Vespasian are brothers to the stone-cut figures of Saint-Sernin. The hair plastered down in curls over

30 – BUSTS OF SAINTS. LIVES OF SAINTS, END OF THE 11TH CENTURY (LE MANS, MS. 214, F. 33 V.)

intimately concerned with the situation in the Western Mediterranean.

From his native Languedoc the "Toulouse man" spread to the centre. We meet him again some time later at Vic, still restless and ardent and still clad in metal, in cleverly composed frescoes which contrast inexplicably with their environs (Saint-Savin, Brinay) unless we accept their Southern origin. He runs and dances in a way which was then scarcely known north of the Massif Central. He has kept his fiery gaze and idiosyncratic features, and an impassioned air which imbues with a kind of violence the touching scenes of the Fall and the Redemption. Few passages in French medieval painting can equal the Kiss of Judas in the almost monochrome frescoes at Vic, with its triangle of figures stretched high up towards the pale face of Christ and its atmosphere of trembling, yet motionless agitation. This penetration of the North by the South might be questioned if the evidence was confined to Vic; but it is confirmed by a group of manuscripts from the Abbey of La Couture, now at Le Mans. They are illustrated by large historiated initials of a kind unknown in the district of the Loire and—even more significantly—by a frieze of quarter-length figures of saints whose relationship with Vic, Toulouse and the Byzantine art of the Mediterranean beyond seems to be established by more than one likeness that is too close to be accidental (Fig. 30). At Le Mans also—a further proof—the Ascension window in the Cathedral (*circa* 1145) was obviously inspired by the Sacramentary of Saint-Étienne, Limoges.

And so the art of the Midi reached and even crossed the Loire. In the West it was to make the essential contribution to the formation of Romanesque painting in Anjou. At the important Abbey of Saint-Aubin, Angers, artistic activity had not entirely ceased during the preceding decades, as we know from the drawings in a Terence and a *Lives of the Bishops of Angers* referred to above. Burnt to the ground in 1032, the abbey was forced to rebuild (a single great tower, isolated in the centre of the town, still survives from these new buildings), and doubtless to make good some part of its library. Abbot Gerard (1082–1108) called in a layman named Fulk who undertook, in return for the gift of a house for life, to paint the whole abbey, to execute its stained-glass windows and, in general, to do whatever work was required of him. The windows and murals of Saint-Aubin disappeared along with the abbey itself during the 18th century, but the books illustrated in Gerard's time and the frescoes at Château-Gontier, a dependency of Saint-Aubin, are in all probability by Fulk. In any case a new art appeared in Anjou at this date, akin to the murals at Saint-Savin, to a *Life of St. Radegund* from her monastery at Poitiers (Fig. 31), and also to the frescoes at Vic.

Vic, Poitiers and Saint-Savin are linked to the South and to Catalonia. Angevin painting is therefore a Southern enclave in Carolingian territory. This explains the strange and severe style of the Bible of Saint-Aubin, of its Psalter and of the *Life* of its patron saint; wholly foreign to this region, it was perhaps introduced by Fulk, the itinerant painter whose contract exactly coincides with its appearance. The immense full-page Christ in Majesty of the Bible stands out against a background of bare parchment, its gigantic height emphasized by the smallness of the head. The stiff folds, flat as if they had been ironed, remove all sense of volume, all appearance of corporeality; but the face is gentle and calm and the expression profoundly human: a contrast which the artist deliberately sought, combining infinite goodness with infinite power. Nobility of poise and feature also distinguishes the holy King David from his four musicians, who are heavier and closer to ordinary humanity (Fig. 32). Again, in the *Life of St. Albinus* (Pl. xx) there is a contrast between the intellectual gifts and moral authority of the saint and the vulgarity of the guests sitting down to a feast given to celebrate an incestuous marriage; and there is a like contrast between the splendid Norman soldiers drawn up in regular ranks on the deck of their ship and the disorderly rabble of the men of Guérande, who however routed them thanks to the protection of St. Albinus.

The drive to the North did not stop there. We may hesitate to attribute to Southern infiltration the nervous quality of the evangelists painted at Corbie at the end of the 11th century; the influence is perhaps that of Rheims and England (Pl. xxii). But the singular analogies between the Josephus from Toulouse and a late 11th-century *Life of St. Audomarus* seem to reveal southern influences on the very borders of France. There is a violence wholly foreign to Saint-Bertin and a taste for relief which at that date only the Midi could, however laboriously, express—evident in the trouble the artist takes to mark the frame of his picture and

31 — SS. RADEGUND AND MEDARDUS. LIFE OF ST. RADEGUND, END OF THE IITH CENTURY (POITIERS, MS. 250, F. 27 V.)

32 – DAVID. PSALTER OF ANGERS, END OF THE 11TH CENTURY
(AMIENS, MS. LESCALOPIER 2, F. 11⁵ V.)

In the preceding pages an attempt has been made to sketch in outline the varied expressions of French painting during its first century, a long "century" extending from about the year 1000 to the year 1130. It undoubtedly had its share of successes, even of masterpieces, but borrowing was the order of the day. The 12th century is less easy to analyse. It was the period of Romanesque maturity, and though borrowing continued as in the 11th century, the sources were fewer and the decorative capital accumulated from all sides could be drawn upon at leisure. Groups were formed which seem to be autonomous but cannot easily be analysed. English influence ceased, at least for a time; the same was true of Italy; and German influence entered only by way of the Meuse. It was the Mediterranean that now chiefly enriched French art—Byzantium and her dependencies and the classical tradition she inherited. The cause, as much perhaps as the Crusades, was the revival of interest in the culture of the Eastern Mediterranean in all its aspects (witness the schools of translators established at Palermo, at Constantinople and in Spain) and the closer and more direct contacts in art, literature and science, which culminated in the theological and moral conclusions of the *Summa* of St. Thomas Aquinas.

This movement began early, at Rheims. There, throughout the Middle Ages, art was continuously inspired by Antiquity. Many of its different aspects were imitated, by the painters of Archbishop Ebbo's Gospel-book in the 9th century as in the 13th-century Visitation in the Cathedral. The tendency may be explained by the presence of numerous Gallo-Roman remains on what had been the site of the ancient metropolis of Belgica Secunda. To mention only one of several manuscripts, a late 11th-century Lectionary given to the Cathedral before 1096 by its provost Manasses contains initials with figures obviously borrowed from the classical repertoire and recognisable as such in spite of some Romanesque reworking: a beater armed with an axe and blowing a horn; a huntsman pursuing a monster; a young man crowned with leaves; and a servant offering his master a cup of wine, in illustration of Christ's saying, "No man can serve two masters" (Pl. XXIII).

immediately to make his figures overlap it on all sides (Pl. XXI). It is true that the stiff, fluted draperies, so typical of the Southern style, are not without parallels in Mosan painting. A sacramentary from Liège, adapted for Saint-Bertin, perhaps explains the dress of St. Audomarus's companions. But it lacks the essential quality, the frenzy of the South.

We may add that our hypothesis is substantiated by a fact. In 1084 Baldwin I, Count of Boulogne and Guines, on a pilgrimage to Santiago de Compostella, stopped at the Cluniac Abbey of Charroux, which lies north-west of Limoges in the territory of Aquitaine, and was struck by the order and discipline of the monastery. He had recently founded an abbey at Andres, in his native Morinie, and thither he brought monks from Charroux, one of whom he appointed abbot. A flow of gifts to the new community followed the Southern monks, and they were confirmed by Gerard, Bishop of Thérouanne, the seat in those days of the modern bishopric of Saint-Omer.

The Midi

A Bible made for the Abbey of Saint-Martial, Limoges, about 1100 contains Aquitanian interlace which recalls Albi; its precise and dynamic style is reminiscent of Toulouse; and the lively colouring, together with certain decorative themes, comes from Saint-Sever-sur-Adour. But the painters of this magnificent work, one of the masterpieces of French Romanesque painting, infinitely surpass their predecessors. Their use of a regular geometric framework, which we can easily reconstruct, results in a new harmony and equilibrium (Pl. XXVI). The slender proportions of the figures and the discreet stylization give to their pictures an elegance which we can only compare, although it is less cold, to that of the second style of Cîteaux (see below). As at Cîteaux, though earlier, classicism—derived perhaps from Mozarabic Spain—permeates the whole work. Most of the columns, in the Canon Tables and elsewhere, end in bases and capitals formed by animals or little figures of caryatids and Atlases, crouching or standing, single or in pairs (Fig. 33). Identical figures are to be found in North Italian sculpture at the same date, in the pulpit of Sant' Ambrogio, Milan, and a little later at Verona. How are we to explain the obvious connection between the two? The Italian sculptor must have taken his ideas from beyond the Alps: Italy has given France so much that France can well afford, from time to time, to make her a present in return. It remains to explain the presence of these strange motifs at Limoges; probably, as in the 10th century (see p. 27), they are a Carolingian survival.

The immediate successor of Stephen Harding's witty draughtsman (or of Harding himself; see p. 21) was a painter—one of his manuscripts is dated St. Lawrence's Day, 10th August, 1134—who illustrated for Cîteaux and the Abbey of La Ferté-sur-Grosne a series of books diametrically opposed in character to those of his predecessor. We possess a Lectionary, two volumes of St. Jerome's Commentaries on the Prophets, a copy of St. Gregory's *Moralia*, and a few initials in the Bible of Saint-Bénigne, Dijon, in which he collaborated. Some of his miniatures are justly famous: a Christ surrounded by twelve little prophets, Daniel in the lions' den (Pl. XXIV), and a full-page Virgin and Child (Pl. XXV). Even more than their bare simplicity and their rather forbidding nobility, of which other examples exist from Limoges,

it is their general air of exalted calm and their freedom that gives these paintings their unique character. Life itself animates forms and features alike and renders them more supple and more spiritual, in spite of the extreme firmness of the drawing. It is in fact precisely this firmness that saves them from being mere imitations of the sensible world, although such imitation was from now on to be the goal of every endeavour, through an infinity of detours, fresh starts and repentances. A new age was beginning. In the Lectionary, a Virgin in a Tree of Jesse is labelled "Theotokos", an unambiguous stamp of her origin. Byzantium has declared herself, although there are clear signs of a Mozarabic intermediary. That alone would explain the appearance of Kufic characters in one of the frames; and a general relationship with the Bible of Saint-Martial, and through it with the art of the South-West, leads one to suppose that this Byzantine influence came from the South. The relationship is only a general one, and objects of Oriental origin were very widely available to the artists of the period; so we must be wary, even suspicious, in playing the game of attributions. At Cîteaux in any case, whatever the reason, there was an abrupt break between the first style, that of Harding, and the second. And if at Cluny, as we have seen, the paintings already show signs of Byzantine influence, the decoration of its initials, which leaves no room for interpretation and so can never mislead us, proves that

33 – ATLASES. BIBLE OF SAINT-MARTIAL; LIMOGES, END OF THE 11TH CENTURY (BIBLIOTHÈQUE NATIONALE, MS. LAT. 8, VOL. II, F. 170 V.)

33

34 – THE VIRGIN HOLDING A MEDALLION OF JOB. ST. GREGORY, MORALIA IN JOB, END OF THE 12TH CENTURY (SAINT-OMER, MS. 12, VOL. II, F. 84 V.)

there at any rate the Byzantine influence came through Germany. There is no trace of such influence at Cîteaux or at Saint-Bénigne, where Abbot Jarento (1078–1113) maintained contacts, which resulted in a free exchange of presents, with Raymond, Count of Galicia, the son of William, Duke of Burgundy, and husband of Urraca, Queen of Castille.

The North

In about 1130 and in the years that followed, masters with Mosan affiliations were working at Saint-Bertin. They were no less active than their predecessors in the 11th century. English influence, which had once been so powerful, no longer counted for anything, and the same style prevailed at Floreffe, Averbode and Saint-Bertin, and perhaps also at Hénin-Liétard, unless the delightful Gospel-book which once belonged to that abbey is really a product of Saint-Bertin, of whose style it is a perfect example (Pl. XXIX). The mannerism of a St. Matthew surrounded by half-medallions in the Mosan (and Rhenish) manner is balanced by its severely stylized modelling and its warm and varied colours, daringly juxtaposed. The round faces, the pink patches on the cheeks, and the smiling expressions degenerate in less careful work into inflammation and rictus, where the pigment is applied too thickly and destroys the spontaneity of the drawing.

From Saint-Bertin a number of interesting illuminated manuscripts have survived, and it looks as if already, as in the 15th century, painting had in part become an industry, divided between a draughtsman, who was sometimes excellent (Pl. XXVII), and a more or less competent assistant who painted, and all too often daubed, his compositions. A Bible and a St. Gregory of the late 12th century, for instance, are illustrated by admirable drawings frequently coarsened by heavy paint. Although their technical training was Mosan, the draughtsmen of Saint-Bertin drew freely from the repertoire of Byzantine figures. Their pictures contain sirens, centaurs, huntsmen, wrestlers, sphinxes, monkeys and pairs of beasts facing one another, sometimes "reserved" against the capital of a column—a technique which points to the imitation of reliefs, as in Aquitaine a century earlier.

The painting of Saint-Bertin, therefore, is Mosan in style, but its decorative figures are all of antique origin. Since the beginning of the Middle Ages small ivories, textiles and enamels from the Eastern Mediterranean had entered Europe and had been copied constantly not only in France but throughout the West. The 12th century saw a general intensification of this process. Not only decorative figures but subjects of illustration were imitated. It was from Byzantium that a Saint-Bertin painter, in about 1160, borrowed the idea of showing (at the beginning of

34

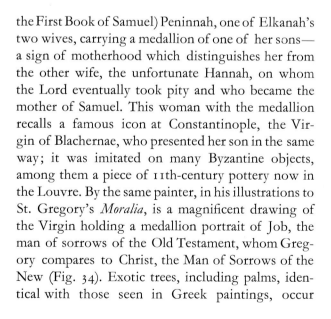

35 – SCENES FROM THE LIFE OF ST. AMANDUS. LIFE OF ST. AMANDUS, SECOND HALF OF THE 11TH CENTURY (VALENCIENNES, MS. 502, F. 29)

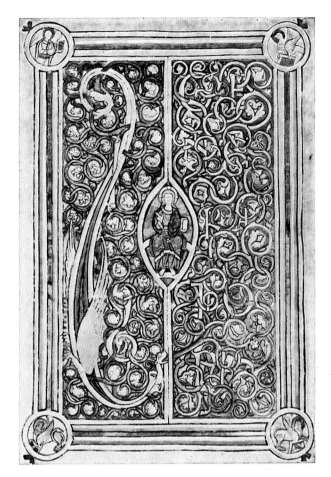

36 – CARPET PAGE. BIBLE OF SAINT-AMAND, SECOND HALF OF THE 12TH CENTURY (VALENCIENNES, MS. 5, F. 16 V.)

the First Book of Samuel) Peninnah, one of Elkanah's two wives, carrying a medallion of one of her sons— a sign of motherhood which distinguishes her from the other wife, the unfortunate Hannah, on whom the Lord eventually took pity and who became the mother of Samuel. This woman with the medallion recalls a famous icon at Constantinople, the Virgin of Blachernae, who presented her son in the same way; it was imitated on many Byzantine objects, among them a piece of 11th-century pottery now in the Louvre. By the same painter, in his illustrations to St. Gregory's *Moralia*, is a magnificent drawing of the Virgin holding a medallion portrait of Job, the man of sorrows of the Old Testament, whom Gregory compares to Christ, the Man of Sorrows of the New (Fig. 34). Exotic trees, including palms, identical with those seen in Greek paintings, occur

in the same volume, another indication of the oriental origin of these motifs.

Imitations such as these were purely formal and superficial, though better was to come. The same was true of the other abbeys in the same district, which formed between them a kind of group that must now be examined: Corbie, in Picardy, whose painting at this date has nothing in common with that of earlier times (see p. 30), Marchiennes, Anchin and Saint-Amand, in Hainault.

The artistic activity of Corbie is spread over some thirty years, from the time of Abbot Robert (1123–1142) until 1164, the date of what seems to be the latest surviving manuscript. To begin with it was scarcely brilliant: the scribe took precedence over the decorator and he alone counted. He was named; he was depicted in the frontispiece or in an initial, of-

37 – PETER LOMBARD. SENTENCES, SECOND HALF OF THE 12TH
CENTURY (VALENCIENNES, MS. 186, F. 2 V.)

fering his work to the author of the book or to
St. Peter, the patron of the Abbey (Pl. xxx). The
painters, of whom there were a number, are little superior to the mediocre assistants who coloured the
miniatures of Saint-Bertin, but unlike that of the
latter their work is not redeemed by the quality of
the drawing. The twin abbeys of Marchiennes and
Anchin, on the other hand, possessed first-class artists
who excelled in their decorative initials (though less
conspicuously elsewhere). They lavished upon them
a whole treasury of invention and a rare talent for
drawing and colour. These men appeared on the
scene suddenly, about the middle of the century,
breaking with the modest tradition represented by a
venerable *Life of St. Rictrude*, of the 11th century, and
certain related manuscripts. They had no bonds with
other centres, and appear to have formed their art by
studying antique and Byzantine models, which they
interpreted according to their differing temperaments
and differing degrees of skill. Many of them were at
work together and they were doubtless more or less

exactly contemporary with each other (Pl. xxxi). The
group is interesting enough in itself, but even more
interesting in view of its "open" character. It was
anything but a closed circle and some of its members,
whose names—Siger and Oliver—are, unusually
enough, known to us, were active in the second half
of the century, concurrently with a painter named
Felix who worked at Corbie but was much superior to
his colleagues. These artists foreshadowed in the
plainest possible way the art of the great Bibles (which
will be discussed in a moment), or perhaps they modelled themselves on that art, for it is impossible from
what we at present know to say which (Pl. xxviii).
The Bibles themselves contributed in great measure
to the formation of Gothic art.

The art of these Bibles, which date from the end of
the 12th century, follows on from the art of Corbie,
Marchiennes and Anchin. It can hardly be explained
except as the direct result of Byzantine influence. The
development of painting at Saint-Amand followed
a parallel course. A first *Life of St. Amandus*, of the
second half of the 11th century, has all the general
characteristics of work done at that period in the
neighbouring districts and at the Abbey itself, even
though it is impossible (and pointless) to define their
exact relationship (Fig. 35). The first *Life* served as
model for two others, both much later, and a comparison between the three is all the more interesting
because it reveals certain curious fluctuations.

Soon after 1150 the painter Savalo signed several of
his works, including a copy of St. Hilary of Poitiers
and a Bible of which he illustrated four volumes.
He also decorated a copy of the *Sentences* of Peter
Lombard and part of the second *Life of St. Amandus*.
Each volume of his Bible opens with a whole page
carpeted with ornament. These carpet-pages were
obviously inspired by similar decoration commonly
found in Byzantine manuscripts, especially at Constantinople (Fig. 36). Whether Savalo ever saw
such a manuscript we cannot say, but it is unlikely,
as we know of no Greek illuminated manuscript
entering France in the Middle Ages. More probably the volutes or scrolls, decorated with a plamette
or an acanthus leaf, which characterise his carpet-
pages, came to him from Islamic ivories. But that
does not explain the carpet-pages themselves, and
there is nothing to connect them with those of
the earliest Insular manuscripts, in which the decorative motifs were completely different. All the less so

as Savalo used the same volutes in his initials. Contact with Byzantine decoration and with ivories, and the necessity of using precise contours in order to reproduce the effect of ivories in a drawing, are both perfectly in keeping with the rather heavy firmness of his sure and decisive line, which forms wide, powerful curves, both in his decorated initials and in his portraits, such as that of Peter Lombard (Fig. 37). Savalo failed to take from his Byzantine masters all that he might have, but that was not the case with his successor, who painted the fifth volume of the Bible, decorated a copy of Gilbert de la Porrée, and, most notably, completed the illustrations in the second *Life of St. Amandus*, to which Savalo had contributed only the decorated capital letters (Pl. xxxii). We know nothing of him except that, conscious perhaps of his own originality, he took pains to scratch out his predecessor's initials and to paint them over with patterns of his own; whereas he executed his paintings on the back of previously prepared drawings (Fig. 38) which he preserved and followed closely, not so much out of respect for the artist as for the saint they portrayed. His paintings have a movement, a suppleness and a kind of inward glow which the work of Savalo and of earlier artists at Saint-Amand lacks. These qualities become more clearly defined and at the same time stylised, as happened also in the style of Cîteaux, in the work of a remarkable group of artists, apparently numerous, to whom we owe, at Saint-Amand and elsewhere, a series of paintings as important for the development of Romanesque art as those of the Burgundian abbey. They had understood their lesson and had allowed themselves to be saturated with the teaching of Byzantium, for at that period it is from Byzantium alone that such teaching could have come. And eventually they passed beyond the stage of copying and learnt to understand the very spirit of their models. This can be seen in a famous portrait of St. Gregory, which need only be looked at closely in order to appreciate its hidden laws (Pl. xxxiii). The draperies hug the limbs so that the cloth is stretched tightly over them. The tight folds, calligraphically but naturally drawn, form long, complementary furrows. The painter has exaggerated the smallness of head, hands and feet in order to accentuate the impression of power conveyed by the figure as a whole. The line of the *pallium* is slightly displaced towards the left of the picture in order to balance the inclination of the head and the arm

38 – SCENES FROM THE LIFE OF ST. AMANDUS. LIFE OF ST. AMANDUS, SECOND HALF OF THE 12TH CENTURY (VALENCIENNES, MS. 500, F. 54)

stretched out to the right, holding the book. The expression on the imperious mask of a face emphasises the superhuman strength of the man who remodelled the liturgy of the West. The portrait was imitated at Marchiennes (*frontispiece*) and at Saint-Martin, Tournai. The Crucifixion in a Sacramentary from Saint-Amand belongs to the same family and may even be by the same artist, but it carries stylization a stage further and tends to be mechanical. The Romanesque concern for decoration asserts itself in the artificial undulations of the draperies, their unnatural fluttering, and the highly schematised anatomy of the Christ (Fig. 39).

We no longer find the masterly simplicity of the St. Gregory in the majestic figures of SS. Mark and John from the Abbey of Liessies—all that remain from a sumptuous book now utterly destroyed. The painter's style is so close to the Bible preserved at

39 — THE CRUCIFIXION. SACRAMENTARY OF SAINT-AMAND, SECOND HALF OF THE 12TH CENTURY (VALENCIENNES, MS. 108, F. 58 V.)

40 — DECORATED INITIAL. ST. AUGUSTINE, WORKS, FIRST HALF OF THE 12TH CENTURY (CAMBRAI, MS. 559, F. 40 V.)

Lambeth Palace, to the Dover Bible (both from Canterbury) and to a Psalter now at Glasgow (from York), that we should perhaps see in it a last sign of the English influence to which this part of Northern France was for so long exposed (Pl. XXXIV). The frames of the paintings are embellished with large acanthus leaves and medallions in the manner of the so-called Winchester School. And there is the same taste as in Lambeth and Dover—alongside appreciable differences in detail—both for a continuous line, enveloping the whole figure and restricting the body and the drapery as if with a metal rim, and for folds bounded by double contours which make them stand out like ropes. The strange rim and the double contours clearly imitate Byzantine formulas, those of the painters of the Macedonian Renaissance in the 9th century, or rather of the ivories which followed their style. This hardening, compared with the portrait of St. Gregory, may be due to some outside influence, and it in no way detracts from the achievement of that painting nor from that of Savalo earlier. A copy of the *Works* of St. Augustine, which may have been decorated for the Abbey of Saint-Sépulcre, Cambrai, shows how far the new formulas had enriched even the technique of ornament, how deeply they had penetrated (Fig. 40). The two volutes with palmettes which form the bow of an *H* (combined with a winged monster of oriental demeanour) recall those of the Byzantine carpet-pages. The elegant fighter with cock's feet is squeezed into a garment whose folds stand out like ropes as at Liessies. And as if to underline the origin of these features certain paintings in the same manuscript take us back in the most striking way to the Middle East itself (Fig 41).

But the great masterpiece of Saint-Amand, coming at the end of a process of evolution whose main outlines have now been traced, is the third *Life* of its

38

patron saint. The painter of the seven miniatures that adorn it has both preserved and rendered more supple the characteristics of his predecessors. From an exaggerated schematism he has escaped into simplicity. He makes delicate use of patterned gold and boldly contrasts different tones, delighting in new and warm harmonies: orange and olive green, bright blue, pink, violet. The attitudes of his figures are varied but never forced, and an atmosphere of elegance (it could be called worldliness, if mannerism were not entirely absent) permeates the whole work, enveloping the figures of the saints who seem to move quite naturally in a luxurious and unreal world of their own (Pl. xxxv).

The second period of Romanesque art reaches in this work its climax and conclusion. New qualities appear: suppleness, expressive faces, animated but calm, and a feeling for a general harmony in which spiritual forces and physical appearances are in equilibrium. There is an intelligent understanding of the classical tradition transmitted by Byzantium. All these are united with a genius which transmutes natural forms into decoration and subjects them to the discipline of the plane. As a precursor of Gothic art this painter has no rival; but although Romanesque art had prepared the soil, Gothic art could not flower until other more compelling motives for change had been brought to bear, along with technical innovations that were to alter the whole course of painting.

Before the new style emerged in a coherent form, at Paris about 1230, a troubled period was to interrupt and disorder the development of painting. The disorder is only apparent, the result not so much of the profound transformation that the art of illumination and art in general underwent, as of our own ignorance of the period, which a closer investigation of its works of art may dispel. Among those works of art, there are few more mysterious, in spite of the excellent studies devoted to them, than the twin groups of large Bibles which date from the end of the 12th century and the first years of the 13th: two different but complementary series. In the first series, some of the Bibles are homogeneous in style, others contain a mixture of styles, and at least two draw their images from the Byzantine repertoire, one without making any changes. The latter Bible, the more interesting of the two, comes in theory from the Abbey of Souvigny, though that abbey received it as a gift only in the first half of the 15th century. Another member of the first

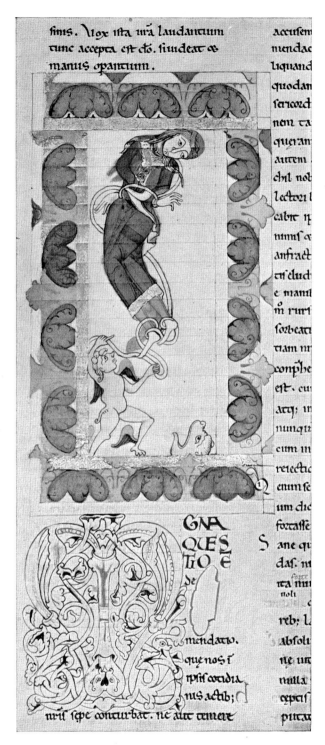

41 – UNTRUTHFULNESS. ST. AUGUSTINE, WORKS, FIRST HALF OF THE 12TH CENTURY (CAMBRAI, MS. 559, F. 73 V.)

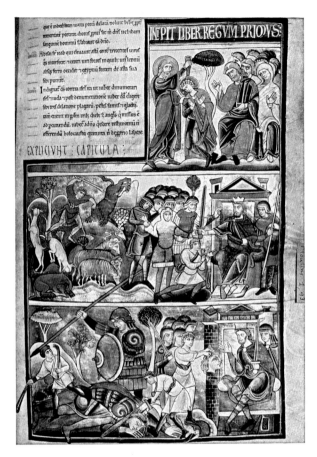

42 – SCENES FROM THE LIFE OF DAVID. SOUVIGNY BIBLE, SECOND HALF OF THE 12TH CENTURY (MOULINS, MS. I, F. 93)

43 – CANON TABLES. PONTIGNY BIBLE, SECOND HALF OF THE 12TH CENTURY (BIBLIOTHÈQUE NATIONALE, MS. LAT. 8823, F. 4 V.)

group, less sumptuous but close to the first in style and iconography, and the only one whose origin is practically certain, comes from Saint-Sulpice, Bourges. The library at Lyon possesses a third, of which Vol. I belongs to the same stylistic family, whereas the figure-painting in Vol. II, impregnated with Byzantine influence from a source other than that of the Souvigny Bible, is the work of an isolated and curiously independent painter. We do not know its origin (Pl. XXXVI). Lastly, there is the Bible presented in 1795 to the library at Clermont-Ferrand, which in pictorial qualities is the most remarkable of the group but again is of unknown origin (Pl. XXXVII).

The power which Byzantium exercised over the artists of these Bibles is plain to see in the Souvigny volume; yet the difference between the Latin spirit and the spirit of the Greek East with its classical heritage is very marked, in spite of the many contacts and the intelligence of the painters at Saint-Amand and elsewhere. Scenes which in the Greek Psalter, now in Paris, are divided into a harmoniously balanced composition in two registers, full of air and life, are in the Souvigny manuscript squeezed into the left half of the lower register. The French artist, using a decorative scheme from which verisimilitude was quite excluded, was less concerned to convey an illusion of life than to suggest the bare facts. Opposite the young David, already trampling on his enemy although he has only that moment discharged the fatal stone, a second Goliath, the stone embedded in his forehead, menaces him with a spear, which, overlapping into the middle register, becomes entangled in the legs of characters unconnected with the fight. The Greek artist, his mind still imbued with antique themes, depicts behind David the Force that upholds him and the Boastfulness of Goliath in

44 – DECORATED INITIAL. BIBLE OF SAINT-ANDRÉ-AU-BOIS,
SECOND HALF OF THE 12TH CENTURY (BOULOGNE, MS. 2, F. 46)

flight: personifications that will have been meaning-
less to a 12th-century Frenchman. Nor is lack of
space enough to explain why the groups of Israelites
and Philistines, a necessary part of the Byzantine
picture, are missing from the Latin Bible; they were
pointless in a scene of which the bare idea was in
itself sufficient and the setting, a battlefield full of
soldiers, superfluous (Fig. 42).

A scribe named Manerius, who describes himself as
a native of Canterbury, signed a Bible in three
volumes now in the Bibliothèque Sainte-Geneviève.
Its illustrations resemble those of a fragment formerly
(in the 18th century) at the Abbey of Pontigny (Fig.
43) and of two other Bibles from Saint-Colombe,
Sens, and Saint-Germain-des-Prés. The Manerius
Bible was purchased in 1748 from the church of
Saint-Loup, Troyes. The origins of this second
group, or its recent origins at least, thus associate

it with the district round Sens, and in particular with
Pontigny, the Cistercian abbey at which Thomas
Becket, Archbishop of Canterbury, took refuge in
1164, and from which his companion Herbert of
Bosham is known to have taken back to England
books painted in a similar style. This second style is
more homogeneous than the first, but the situation
is complicated by the existence of various more or
less intimate links, as yet imprecisely defined, with
two other volumes: the first attributed to Pontigny
itself (obviously cousin to an extraordinarily wild
and violent Bible formerly at Saint-André-au-Bois,
near Saint-Omer; Fig. 44), the second to Saint-
Bertin (Pl. xxxviii), where monks from Canterbury
took refuge at the time of Becket's exile in 1164.
Finally, to complete the confusion, the Bible of
Saint-Germain-des-Prés referred to above and another magnificent Bible, perhaps from Saint-Denis
(Pl. xxxix), possess certain general traits of style
which appear to link them to the first, Byzantinizing
group; and when we consider from this angle the
other Bibles in their group and a number of other
contemporary French manuscripts, we find a striking
uniformity in the initials. Careful scrolls ending in a
large, exuberant acanthus doubled over at the edge
are repeated time and time again, closely resembling
a certain type of Byzantine acanthus of which they
are probably an imitation (Fig. 45).

This uniformity gives us a foretaste of Gothic
uniformity. The ground was slowly, almost in-
sensibly, being prepared, but under what precise
conditions we do not know. They will one day
have to be elucidated. The Abbey of Clairvaux seems
to have played a leading role in the preparations,
which is all the more strange because its founder,
St. Bernard, who died in 1153, had waged an
energetic campaign against the abuse of painted
decoration in manuscripts and had imposed on his
own house, though without securing its adoption
elsewhere, a type of simple initial of the utmost
plainness and severity. Even at Clairvaux, however,
the reform scarcely survived his death. Decoration
reappeared, the same essentially Byzantine decoration
as before, and drawing also, as in the Northern
abbeys at this date. Pontigny and Clairvaux, both
daughter houses of Cîteaux, appear largely respon-
sible for these developments.

And so at the end of the 12th century in France many
roads lead to Byzantium. We must not see her

influence everywhere; yet neither must we ignore the many signs, open and hidden, of her insinuating presence. They are plain to see in form and iconography alike; in the colour-scheme of blue, red and gold which was to dominate Gothic painting; and in the sustained impetus which from the earliest strivings of the 12th century onwards she imparted to the representation of earthly life and to the expression of a new spirituality, both more human and less rigid than before.

45 — ACANTHUS LEAF. LETTERS OF ST. GREGORY, SECOND HALF OF THE 12TH CENTURY (BIBLIOTHÈQUE NATIONALE, MS. LAT. 2287, F. 2)

GOTHIC ILLUMINATION

THE progress of Gothic illumination saw the gradual conquest of the world of sensible appearances–the veil that shrouded the realities with which alone the medieval spirit had hitherto been concerned. Already in the Romanesque period artists had attempted to impart to a flat plane the illusion of space and depth; at the beginning of the 11th century at Toulouse, for example, by an ingenious device which we may best compare to the wings of a stage. But such attempts are rare and uniform. Not until towards the end of the 14th century do we find similar formulas more maturely handled, in the earliest attempts to portray true landscapes and convey an impression of distance. During the first century of French Gothic art—say from 1230 to 1330—the will to escape from the flat plane reveals itself not so much in the modelling of individual figures, which had earlier been understood by the Romanesque artists, as in the search for movement. Forms grow softer and more pliable, though in some cases they are still no more than flat silhouettes; proportion and perspective are now used to portray objects not according to the artist's idea of them, but as they appear to him. Little by little the world is cut down to the human scale, the first stage in a revolution which was only to be completed in the 15th century. Its progress is marked by the gradual development of the background, at first simply a decorative pattern or sketchy outline, later becoming an integral part of the space that the figures and objects occupy, surrounding them and enveloping them in its light or shade. The revolution ended when the spectator felt able to step forward into the interiors created by the painters or to set foot upon the soil of their landscapes, with the horizon at eye level and an open sky above.

The first signs of this spiritual and technical revolution appeared in the second half of the 12th century. The monastic centres of art were, as we have seen, losing their power; they were soon to be wholly or nearly silenced, as if rased to the ground, and none of them ever revived. The arts fell into new hands, as though new teams of artists had long been preparing to succeed the old. Only one explanation is possible: the patrons and clients changed, the artists followed. Art lives on programmes and programmes depend on commissions, on the people who distribute them, whether individuals or officials, single or in groups. Behind every work of art lies the patron who called it into being. At this period the clientele was changing. Everywhere the abbeys and cathedrals were being replaced as centres of learning by the universities, especially the University of Paris, to which scholars flocked from all over Europe; and by an increasing number of patrons for romances, histories, didactic treatises and works of private devotion, of whom the most important was the king. Every French king after St. Louis was an owner of books. Louis himself bequeathed his library to Royaumont and in his lifetime opened it to Vincent de Beauvais, thus assisting the compilation of the gigantic *Speculum* in which that erudite

encyclopedist summed up the learning of his time.
The distant journeys of the Crusades, the discovery
of Greek and Arabic science, and the social changes
provoked by the establishment of communes and
the emergence of a mercantile and financial bour-
geoisie created similar conditions to those which
provoked, for like reasons and with like results, the
Renaissance of the 15th and 16th centuries. The
production of books passed into the hands of the
laity. Round the University of Paris and elsewhere,
to supply a shifting population of teachers, students
and ordinary book-lovers, there sprang up publishing
houses, which gathered together the different
specialists: scribes, correctors, illuminators, some
of whom painted the decoration only, while others

painted figure-subjects or "histories". Illustrators continued to draw their ideas from the whole of the
Latin West, and even from beyond, as they had done
in Romanesque times and as the University itself
did in another sphere. But whereas the Romanesque
period was purely receptive, French Gothic art
exports; it takes the ideas of others and marries them
to its own, but what emerges is French and bears an
unmistakable stamp of its origin.

Let us now consider who the new patrons and cus-
tomers were, what changes they provoked, and how
they were carried out. Everywhere the abbeys were
in decline, and although certain northern houses were
to carry on an honourable existence for some time
longer, only Saint-Denis, the royal abbey, produced an important artistic innovation. Its most
distinguished Abbot was Suger (1082–1152), counsellor to the king and regent of France from 1147 to
1150 during Louis' absence in the Holy Land; and
he was, if not the creator, at least a promoter of what
he himself calls the "new style" of architecture and
stained glass. He has described his activities in a
treatise which is all the more precious because it does
not simply list his own works. It explains how the
new methods of building had made it possible to
reduce the wall-space, to open up broad bays and to
allow a play of light on large windows decorated
with "histories". Earthly brightness could thus be
used to evoke the idea of heavenly brightness.

A sparkling tapestry, the stained glass window
replaced the fresco, for which the dwindling of the
wall-space left less and less room; and thanks to the
material and spiritual importance which they assumed
under the auspices of architectural technique, the
windows took the lead in pictorial art, of which
they are themselves a variant. The illuminators, or
at least those of the new workshops, set themselves
to learn from the windows, upon which they modelled their composition, their iconography, their
colours, their forms, and even, in spite of certain
necessary differences, their technique. So much so
that on occasion illumination and stained glass
seem to be the work of the same artists. We say
"seem", cautiously, since all we lack is proof, the
name of a single artist who worked both on books
and in glass. Yet how are we to explain the strange
series of pictures in the *Life of Christ* in the Pierpont
Morgan Library, New York (Fig. 46), except as the
work of one of the artists of the windows at Chartres

44

(*circa* 1150–60) or at least of a pupil (the manuscript is possibly later), so closely does it resemble the Life of Christ in the west window at Chartres. From one to the other, style and iconography are indistinguishable.

The fabrication of a window presupposes the preparation of a design in the form of a painted cartoon, and in the manuscript—which consists of a single (and complete) gathering of sixteen leaves with a blank page at either end—we possess what must be a designer's pattern-book. The windows at Chartres were inspired by the windows at Saint-Denis, and the new style of illumination, which owed so much to stained glass and which the little pattern-book with its linear modelling and unbroken colours so clearly foreshadows, was formed in a milieu which resembled, and may perhaps have been identical with, the royal abbey. After the thick paint and general softness of Romanesque art in decline, painting needed the discipline of clean, dry line and of light boldly distributed over large, plain surfaces. It was precisely this discipline that stained glass had to offer, and it may well be that the small but well-placed group of artists who manned the new workshops were partly recruited from the cartoonists. At the end of the 15th century, when illumination had lost its decorative quality and approximated to panel-painting, engravers were recruited from the designers of cartoons for embroidery. A development of the same sort in the second half of the 12th century would account for one of the technical changes which transformed the art of painting in the 13th. The *Life of Christ* points to a connection of this sort; the imposing *Bible moralisée* executed about 1250 in the royal workshops and, even more emphatically, the Psalter of St. Louis confirm it.

The Bible (Pl. xl) marks the completion of a change which had begun in the middle of the 12th century. It is neither more nor less than a set of stained glass windows transposed on to parchment. The thick volumes contain nothing but historiated medallions disposed in groups of eight, and each of the painted openings forms a diptych separated from its neighbours by a pair of empty pages. The medallions are arranged in pairs and are explained by an inscription at the side; one represents a scene from the Bible, the other contains a picture which reveals its moral significance. Typology—the comparison of events

47 – THE MACCABEES. LA NOBLE CHEVALERIE DE JUDAS MAC-CHABÉE, 1285 (BIBLIOTHÈQUE NATIONALE, MS. FR. 15104, F. 26 v.)

in the Old Testament with events which they prefigured in the New—here gives way to moralising, which is more didactic, better suited to the public for whom the Bible was intended. The enormous labour presupposed by the decoration of this monumental work, of which several copies were produced, must have been equalled by the no less considerable labour of making extracts from the text and its moral commentary, which comes from the *Postillae in Bibliam* of Hugues de Saint-Cher, a Dominican who died in 1262. The task must have required a learned director, assisted by scribes and painters, and considerable funds. It is thought that another Dominican, Vincent de Beauvais, may have been asso-

45

ciated with the work—he was not one to take fright at the sight of a long job; but that is no more than a conjecture, and there seems to be no reason why Hugues de Saint-Cher himself should not have had a hand in the methodical plagiarising of his own text. There still exist three copies of the Bible, of which the best, the royal copy, is at Toledo and New York. A fragment of the French translation is at Vienna. It is in the same style, possibly even by the same artists as a Gospel-lectionary for the Sainte-Chapelle in Paris (circa 1260–70). This lectionary, which was executed at two different dates, is in its latter part—completed some ten years later—the work of artists who are even more certainly associated with the crown. They are the authors of a splendid Psalter, also for use in the Sainte-Chapelle, which was executed for St. Louis after 1253 and doubtless little before his death in 1270 (Pl. XLII).

The manuscript begins with a series of 78 full-page paintings in front of the text, portraying scenes from the Old Testament from the offering of Cain and Abel to the Coronation of Saul (several of the early scenes are missing); they face one another in pairs, and on the back of each page is simply an explanatory inscription. The elements of the style are still Romanesque, but it is animated by a new spirit. The liveliness, the elegant proportions, the supple forms with their tendency towards a slightly stylized realism, the warm but harmonious colours, enriched by the gold of the backgrounds—all these give to the work a youthful, springtime quality. The trefoil arches and architectural features which surmount each scene, with the thin columns which divide them as occasion demands, are the only element in the miniatures which is Gothic in the full sense of the word. They are a faithful reproduction of the arcades, gables and rose windows of the Sainte-Chapelle, and it seems as if we must certainly recognise in them the directing hand of St. Louis' architect, Pierre de Montreuil, perhaps even the personal intervention of the king. Nothing of the kind had been seen before. It was in the entourage of St. Louis that French Gothic art, and especially painting, had its true origin.

Somewhat later, about 1285, are two treatises (the first dated) illustrated by an illuminator who comes possibly from the northern part of the Ile-de-France, if not from Paris itself: the *Noble chevalerie de Judas Machabée* and a copy of the Bestiary as translated by Guillaume le Clerc. They show that illumination was still closely dependent on stained glass, although it was not to remain so for very long. Thick black lines, all very firmly drawn, surround the various colours like the lead in a window, and modelling is achieved as in glass, whether plain or coloured, by means of delicate grisaille. The illuminator was too well acquainted with stained glass not to have been a master glazier, or at least a designer accustomed to preparing cartoons for windows (Fig. 47). It is enough to examine the section devoted to "portraiture" in the collection of plans, designs and models made by the architect Villard de Honnecourt, in about 1250, to be certain that his system of "portraiture" reproduces the system used in the contemporary *Bible moralisée*. The geometrical framework used is one on which balanced compositions can be rapidly and easily constructed—a device which has a long history and was well known to the Romans. The techniques of the architect and of the painter had combined (Fig. 48).

The influence of stained glass was not in itself enough to form Gothic illumination; artists drew from other sources the material to develop it. To

48 – THE WHEEL OF FORTUNE. SKETCHBOOK OF VILLARD DE HONNECOURT, MIDDLE OF THE 13TH CENTURY (BIBLIOTHÈQUE NATIONALE, MS. FR. 19093, F. 21 V.)

begin with, naturally enough, they retained the grammar of late Romanesque ornament, as we find it in the great Bibles of the late 12th century described earlier. It would be easy to point to these same features in a number of illuminated manuscripts dating from the first half of the 13th century, the most important of which are no longer Bibles but Psalters. A change was already under way. The Bible, which in those days was often of enormous size, was the fundamental reference-book of the monks, a work which every abbey possessed and which was sometimes magnificently decorated. The Psalter, which replaced it as the *livre de luxe*, was intended for laymen, and no surviving example is bigger than a large modern octavo. It was for use in private devotions, and in the form in which it appears at the beginning of the 13th century was the precursor of the Book of Hours, which entirely superseded it for that purpose towards the end of the 14th century. Psalters of this kind were an English invention; or at any rate the English, in the second half of the 12th century, brought them to a pitch of sumptuous perfection unknown in France.

Of the Psalters that have survived one of the most valuable for the history of French illumination is in the University Library at Leyden. It was written at the end of the 12th century for Geoffrey Plantagenet, who was Archbishop of York from 1191 to 1212, and must have fallen into the hands of Philip Augustus's son Louis when he crossed the channel to assist the barons in their revolt against King John. It is supposed that Louis gave it to his wife Blanche of Castille; and that it was thus that the young St. Louis came to learn his letters from it, as we discover from a note added to the volume at the beginning of the 14th century. Thus there entered France, through the medium of the royal family, a style of decoration which Parisian artists were quick to copy and which inspired a fine series of Psalters dating from the first half of the 13th century. The English style was, however, modified by contact with the new Parisian art.

There is as yet no sign of this modification in the magnificent Psalter painted for the unfortunate Ingeburga of Denmark, after her desertion by Philip Augustus. This volume dates if not from the last years of the 12th century, since Ingeburga was repudiated immediately after her marriage in 1193, at least from the first two decades of the 13th, when she was more

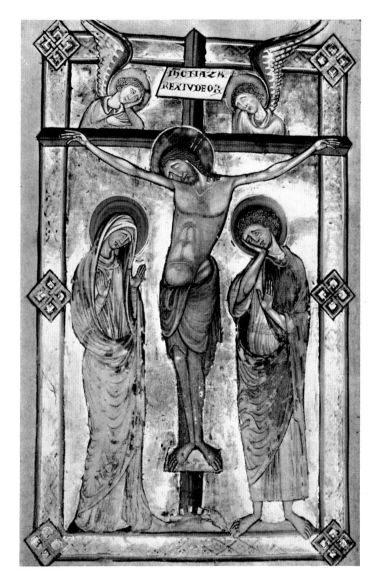

49 – THE CRUCIFIXION. MISSAL OF ANCHIN, CIRCA 1200 (DOUAI, MS. 90, F. 98 V.)

or less restored to favour. Although a Psalter of Paris use compiled for the Queen of France, it has nothing Parisian about its illumination, nor English either. The painter, like Ingeburga herself, came from beyond the Rhine, and until we know more we must be content to look for parallels to its radiant pictures and light, fresh colours among the still distinguished posterity of the Ottonians. The Psalter has rightly been compared with a Missal from Anchin (Fig. 49), but that too seems to be foreign and was probably imported by the Ingeburga painter.

On the other hand—a sign of the change that was already taking place in Europe—the royal workshop in Paris, that of the *Bible moralisée*, undertook about 1230 to decorate the Psalter of Princess Christina, daughter of Haakon Haakonson, King of Norway, who in 1258 married Philip, brother of Alfonso X of Castille and Leon and nephew of St. Louis' mother. From now on *livres de luxe* were to come from Paris. Several other Psalters, of which one is ascribed without complete proof to Blanche of Castille, contain introductory miniatures in superimposed series of medallions, a device which the illuminators had borrowed from stained glass (Pls. XLII, XLIV). The style of this workshop appears elsewhere: for instance in a *Liber Floridus*—prose anthology—by Lambert of Saint-Omer (Pl. XLV). By about 1250 the new style had assumed its final, even its most extreme form. It was strictly linear and flat. It employed wide areas of warm colour, mostly deep red and blue, on which modelling was indicated by over-painting in black or in another shade of the same colour. Faces were not coloured, and features and hair were indicated by simple strokes of the pen. This extreme aridity, or—if you prefer it—this deliberate, rather forced legibility, so completely opposed to the last excesses of Romanesque painting, was at that time the hallmark of Paris. It is found in the Bible from the royal workshop, in the Psalters, in the Gospel-lectionary of the Sainte-Chapelle (Fig. 50), and also in lay books—fables, prose or verse romances, and histories—to which this somewhat schematic form of illustration was perfectly suited. Examples are the *Roman de Troie* by Benoît de Saint-More, the *Histoire de Jérusalem* by Guillaume de Tyr, the *Conte de Méliacin* by Girard d'Amiens, and the *Roman de la Poire* (Pl. XLVI), all of which date roughly from between 1250 and 1275.

During the 13th century, the style of Paris was diffused throughout France, in step with the increasing centralisation of political power. No longer is French painting divided into two more or less equal halves, as in the Romanesque period: the North has the upper hand, and where a Southern style does appear, it is a thinly veiled version of the Northern or of the Italian style (or Spanish, although

50 – THE GOOD SHEPHERD. GOSPEL LECTIONARY OF THE SAINTE-CHAPELLE, CIRCA 1260–1270 (BIBLIOTHÈQUE NATIONALE, MS. LAT. 17326, F. 99)

Spain, or to be more precise Catalonia, was in this respect a province of Italy). The Gothic of the Ile-de-France dominated the whole stage, and from this we may infer that the Ile-de-France possessed a virtual monopoly of illumination, a monopoly which it shared in part, as we shall see, with other secondary centres.

It is probable that painters travelled about and hired themselves out to execute commissions on the spot, as Fulk had done earlier at Saint-Aubin, Angers; but, unfortunately, we know of only one example. In 1317, Everard, a monk of the monastery of Froid-mont, near Beauvais, was superintending the compilation of a pocket Breviary for the use of his abbot, and he entrusted its decoration to "master John of Amiens, then resident at Beauvais". But for a note in the manuscript recording this detail, we should be entitled to believe that the Breviary was not only written but decorated at Froidmont; and yet the painter was in fact a layman *(magister)*, whose home was certainly at Amiens (his style is the style of Picardy), and who was working at Beauvais for the time being *(tunc temporis)*, which plainly shows that his residence there was only temporary. Everard simply took the opportunity which was offered him. Nothing demonstrates more clearly how important it is to dissociate the writing of a book from its decoration. Because a text comes from a particular abbey, it does not necessarily follow that it was also decorated there. We know nothing of the living and working conditions of the painters of the period, but it seems obvious that a painter can only have been trained in an artistic centre, amidst other painters, and that few such centres can have existed; the unity of Gothic art points to this.

There is another detail to note in the Froidmont Breviary. Like innumerable other volumes, it contains a note for the illuminator, telling him what subject to portray in the single historiated initial: "li abes qui cante se messe", the abbot singing his Mass. This note was certainly written by Everard, who commissioned the miniature, not by the head of a workshop, who would more probably have made a sketch for himself or his client to follow. We must not imagine the workshops as so many little factories scattered over the country, each with a head man who distributed tasks to its workmen. Successful illuminators might set up shop as regular suppliers to publishing houses or to the great book-

51 – THE TRINITY: SPORTS AND PASTIMES. PARIS CHANSONNIER, CIRCA 1280–1315 (MONTPELLIER, BIBLIOTHÈQUE DE LA FACULTÉ DE MÉDECINE, MS. 196, F. 87 V.)

collectors, employing assistants and entering into partnerships; but a Jean d'Amiens worked single-handed or nearly so, travelling about from town to town and taking his own style and technique wherever he went.

We know of one of these employers, Maître Honoré of the Rue Erembourg-de-Brie (Boutebrie), Paris. He appears in a tallage roll for the year 1296. That same year the accounts of the treasury at the Louvre mention that a Breviary belonging to Philip the Fair was illuminated by one Honoré. That both documents refer to the same man, we know from a copy of Gratian's *Decretum*, which was purchased from the illuminator Honoré, Rue Boutebrie, in 1288 and contains a miniature by the hand that illustrated the king's Breviary.

49

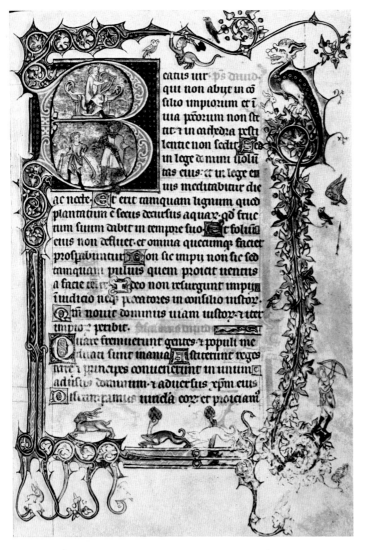

52 – DECORATED PAGE. BREVIARY OF SAINT-SÉPULCRE; CAMBRAI, CIRCA 1290 (CAMBRAI, MS. 102, F. 232)

curving inwards at the top and outwards below, lead the eye towards the luminous figure of the young David, who is the chief character in each scene, as an inscription in capital letters which refers to both registers informs us; the angel, in the upper register, offsets the towers of Bethlehem, maintaining the balance of the picture, as do the trees which suggest a landscape in the lower. A subtle art, which reveals its secrets only on analysis, its restraint and calm enhances its effect, although there are, we must admit, a few concessions to formula—in the movements of legs and feet and in the arched brows, high bulging foreheads, tense expressions and carefully curled hair. It contained the seeds of future developments, even of the touch of mannerism which Honoré's successors did not always avoid, and which, kept within reasonable bounds, was long to remain one of the distinguishing marks of Parisian illumination. Of the works contemporary with Honoré, the Martyrology of Saint-Germain-des-Prés, whose peasants have their hair nicely curled and wear the most elegant rags, has been mentioned. There is also a witty *Chansonnier* from Paris, whose pages are enlivened by gay marginal scenes of sports and pastimes (Fig. 51).

The *Chansonnier* is one of the oldest examples of these *marginalia*. They were soon to be all the rage. The fashion began in quite a small way in the North of France, perhaps in imitation of the English, and artists from the North certainly had a hand in the decoration of the *Chansonnier*. The Trinity on f. 87 v. is in the style of Arras, and unless the volume was decorated in the provinces for use in Paris, which seems to be out of the question in view of the importance of Paris and the ease with which commissions could be executed there, we can only suppose that Northern artists were already establishing themselves in the capital, attracted by the market which it provided for their work. It is natural that working painters, and even publishers, should have brought with them to Paris a manner which was their own particular speciality.

After Honoré, the workshop in the Rue Boutebrie was controlled by his son-in-law Richard de Verdun. We cannot attribute anything to him with certainty, but for want of a better hypothesis it is reasonable to suppose that he carried on the traditions of his father-in-law. They can be detected, in a drier form and with backslidings into the linearity from which

Honoré was a painter of decisive and vigorous talent, whose style, in its precise and discreet elegance, resembles that of a Martyrology painted about 1270 for Saint-Germain-des-Prés (Pl. XLVII), which is therefore unquestionably of Parisian origin. His art epitomizes all that was best in 13th-century France: movement, colour, compact but airy composition. Take, for instance, his frontispiece to the Breviary of Philip the Fair (Pl. XLVIII). The upper register, the more crowded of the two, is exactly the same height as the lower, but the latter, as it is emptier, appears higher and so lightens the whole page. In both registers, the attitudes of the figures,

Honoré himself had liberated French painting, in a series of books which crowded the Parisian market, and were doubtless widely imitated elsewhere, until 1330 and even later (Pls. XLIX, LII). Simple, decorative work, it quickly becomes stereotyped. Some of the books are produced *en masse*, like the many copies of a work then much in demand, the *Bible historiale* of Guiart des Moulins, a French translation of the *Historia Scholastica* of Petrus Comestor; others are of a higher quality, like the *Vie de saint Denis* by the monk Yves, which was presented, also in 1317, to Philip the Tall (Pl. L).

It is interesting to compare the two volumes, both identical in style, dated the same year and possibly from the same workshop, the one intended for the average buyer, the other for a great collector, the King in person (the *Vie de saint Denis* had been prepared for Philip the Fair, a client of Honoré). Allowing for differences in quality, there is a perfect identity between the two and they may well be the work of a single painter. Nothing could be more typically Parisian than this *Life* of the patron saint of Paris, decorated for the King under the supervision of a monk of Saint-Denis. Beneath the main subjects of each miniature are a series of little scenes of Parisian life placed in urban settings which are more or less true to life. They have a touching quality; the first of the long line of Paris painters was inspired by a friendly and amused curiosity for the life of the streets and the river, and for the tradesmen, craftsmen, hucksters, merchants and other humble people who made their noisy and picturesque way through the streets of what was in those days the capital city of Christendom. Paris was the largest city of the age and seemed like the meeting-place of the universe, *orbis in urbe*, in every sphere of activity; it had long been the headquarters of theology and secular learning, and from now on it was to be the headquarters of the arts. The *École de Paris* was founded in the 14th century.

We have noted the importance to Paris and the surrounding district of contacts with the North of France and England. Links with Italy were soon to be established. But before examining them we must turn briefly to the French provinces and discover what they derived from the Paris. The answer is quite simple: everything they possessed. From north to south Paris dominated France, her mastery disputed by Italy only in the Papal city of Avignon

and in Languedoc, which lay on the borders of Catalonia, a country steeped in Italian art. The supremacy of Paris, however, admitted of nuances which enable us to recognize certain regional peculiarities, although they dwindled away to nothing during the 14th century, not to reappear until the second half of the 15th century, when Paris, in the aftermath of Charles VI's disastrous reign, had lost her lead in art as in politics. Three provincial centres in particular are worthy of mention. Picardy-Artois, the country of the troubadours and the writers of romances, was the home of a high-spirited school which shared the gaiety of the writers, and like them was not entirely free from the rather dry clarity which had already become a French characteristic. Modelling was reduced to a minimum; only bright colours were used; and faces were left uncoloured, with their features indicated by lines no thicker than a hair, drawn with the pen. Frames ran riot, surmounted by tall architectural motifs picked out with two shades of gold, or projecting into the margin in sprays loaded with entertaining little figures—the *drôleries* which were a feature of Artois and of English decoration (Pl. LI; Fig. 52). The taste for pure line was nowhere more pronounced. The art of

53 – BOETHIUS, PHILOSOPHY; PLATO AND SOCRATES. BOETHIUS, CONSOLATION DE LA PHILOSOPHIE; METZ, FIRST THIRD OF THE 14TH CENTURY (MONTPELLIER, BIBLIOTHÈQUE DE LA FACULTÉ DE MÉDECINE, MS. 43, F. 2)

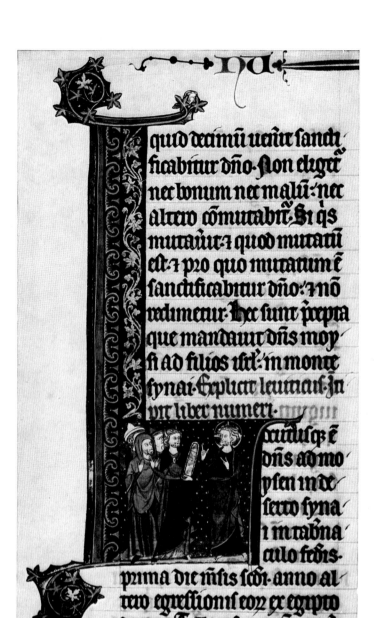

54 — GOD DELIVERS THE LAW TO MOSES. BIBLE OF RHEIMS
CATHEDRAL, BEGINNING OF THE 14TH CENTURY (RHEIMS, MS.
39, F. 99)

Metz was altogether different, with its broken
colours, heavy modelling and stout, solid style,
sometimes a trifle rough but always vigorous, which
spread to Trier and beyond (Fig. 53). Rheims can be
distinguished from Paris only by details which in
many ways recall the simple but majestic decoration
of its own architecture (Fig. 54). Elsewhere in France
there is nothing clear-cut enough to mention in this
rapid survey.

Jean Pucelle

Forty years after Honoré, another Parisian, Jean
Pucelle, established the first French contacts with
Italy. Some notes in a Breviary, which belonged to
the Belleville family and dates from about 1325,
show clearly that Pucelle was head of a firm, paying
wages to his assistants, Mahiet, Ancelot and Chevrier;
and a signature in the bible of Robert de Billyng,
so called after its scribe, confirms that he was, like
his assistants, an illuminator. He was doubtless
well known, even famous; he designed the seal of
the Confraternity of Saint-Jacques-aux-Pèlerins,
Paris; and many years later a book which had belonged to Joan of Évreux, wife of Charles IV, 1325
to 1328, was still known as the *Heures de Pucelle*. In
all probability this Hours is to be identified with a
manuscript now in the Cloisters Museum, New
York (Pl. LIV).

Although the Belleville Breviary (Fig. 55) and the Billyng Bible are firmly linked by written evidence, we
cannot say exactly what part Pucelle himself played in
their actual decoration. However, as he was the
head of the workshop, we may fairly ascribe to him
the responsibility and the credit; and if the so-called
Hours of Joan of Évreux is entirely by his hand, as
seems probable, it is surely no coincidence that it
dominates the whole group and shows the touch of
a master. The head of the workshop owed it to
himself to take personal charge of a volume intended
for the Queen of France; for the other manuscripts
he employed assistants. In addition to the Hours of
Joan of Évreux, we possess six other books executed
between about 1330 and 1355 for ladies of the royal
family related to Joan herself: her sister-in-law,
Joan of Navarre; the latter's cousin, Joan of Savoy
(d. 1344); Blanche of Burgundy, aunt of Joan of
Navarre and wife of Edward, Count of Savoy
(d. 1348; her book was destroyed by fire in the
library at Turin in 1904); and Yolanda of Flanders,
who became Joan's mother-in-law in 1353. For Joan
herself the workshop painted another Breviary, and
for the church of Saint-Louis, Poissy, a Missal.
Also from this workshop are an illustrated copy of
the Trial of Robert of Artois (1336; Fig. 56) and
a fine *Miracles de Notre-Dame*. There still exist many
copies of the latter, a verse work compiled at the
beginning of the 13th century by Gautier de Coincy,
Prior of Vic-sur-Aisne. This particular copy was

made for a member of the royal family, perhaps Joan of Burgundy (d. 1330), the wife of Philip of Valois; lost by John at the battle of Poitiers in 1356, it was ransomed by Charles V. The style derives in its essentials from that of Honoré: subtly cadenced composition, the features and expressions of the faces, excellent modelling obtained almost exclusively by the use of colour, in fresh, lively tones which were unknown to Honoré himself, and even to Pucelle, who preferred a more subdued range of colours (Pl. LIII).

The kalendar of the Belleville Breviary, which is of Dominican use, enjoyed great popularity as a model. Its most original illustrations, the subjects of which are taken from the Kalendar and the Psalter, were planned to form a concordance between the Old and the New Testament. The Virgin Mary, who opened the gates of the Heavenly Jerusalem to mankind, stands on one of the gates of Paradise; in her hand she holds a banner representing one of the articles of Faith upon which the Church was founded; and St. Paul shows it to a recipient of his Epistles. Below, one of the twelve Apostles draws up the articles of the Creed in accordance with the Prophets: it is as though stones were taken from the nearly ruined Synagogue to build the Church. This scheme was imitated in the Hours of Joan of Navarre and the Hours of Yolanda of Flanders, both from Pucelle's own workshop; in the *Petites Heures* and the *Grandes Heures* of John, Duke of Berry; in the Breviary of Martin of Aragon (*circa* 1403); and lastly in a Book of Hours executed about 1425, perhaps for Charles VII and his wife Mary of Anjou. A Breviary which belonged to Charles V contains a similar arrangement (Pl. LV).

Jean Pucelle has been credited with introducing to the Paris workshops marginal decoration, or "drôleries"; in fact they had reached Paris in the early years of the century, coming from Northern France and England, by way of Picard artists in the capital, as the *Chansonnier* at Montpellier shows us. Pucelle, however, certainly improved them, for in his work they are related to the text and often develop or complete some detail of the principal scene. Thus in the *Petites Heures* the figures in the Annunciation to the Shepherds are scattered all over the page; the Massacre of the Innocents prolongs the Adoration of the Magi; the Fall of the Idols and the Pursuit of the Holy Family by Herod's Soldiers complete the representa-

55 – SAUL AND DAVID; CAIN AND ABEL; THE EUCHARIST; CHARITY. BELLEVILLE BREVIARY, CIRCA 1323–1326 (BIBLIOTHÈQUE NATIONALE, MS. LAT. 10484, F. 24 V.)

tion of the Flight into Egypt. Marginal decoration is integrated with the illustration of the book as a whole although for a long time yet there appear the grotesque but amiable monsters (Fig. 57) and the acrobats inherited from the Romanesque repertoire; or—as in the Picard Psalter in the Bibliothèque Nationale and in the *Chansonnier* at Montpellier, whose links with Picardy are obvious—scenes of country and family life, particularly the sports and pastimes of young people, drawn from everyday life but softened and transformed into graceful, decorative arabesques.

Pucelle's great innovation was that he looked towards Italy. But as the heir to Honoré and his formulas, although freer in movement and composition and more restrained in colouring (his masterpiece is in grisaille), he was too Parisian, or at least too French

il ne sont pas nains si come il convient sccor. mais sondre est en soufler precheux.

i ne sont pas prins si come il convient sccor. mais sondre est en soufler precheux.

56 – THE TRIAL OF ROBERT OF ARTOIS. 1336 (BIBLIOTHÈQUE NATIONALE, MS. FR. 18437, F. 2)

and so too far from the spirit of the transalpine masters, to understand their feeling for volume, unique in its day, and to succumb to its influence. His imitation was confined to superficial copying: to reproducing with conscientious skill their architectural decoration, which in his own work merely served as an embellishment. He simply followed the fashion.

As Honoré's successor, Jean Pucelle perfected the qualities which Honoré himself derived from the Parisian tradition: an alert and smiling elegance which could none the less express the gravity of certain scenes. Without being an innovator in the true sense, Pucelle was the first Parisian to attempt a synthesis of the kind that the Limbourg Brothers achieved, on a more complex scale, at the beginning of the 15th century. He took from Italy little more than a method of decoration and a few themes to vary the repertoire of French imagery, but he did at least open the way, and his still timid borrowings served as a basis for the representation of depth, which was gradually to transform illumination and to give modern painting its freedom.

The Painters of John the Good and Charles V

Jean Pucelle was the painter of the first Valois sovereigns. He made his appearance at about the time that Philip IV came to the throne (1328). At this period it was the court, and in particular the ladies of the court, rather than the King in person, that provided the necessary patronage for the *livre de luxe*. However, had John the Good (1350–1364) not spent part of his reign in captivity (1356–1360 and 1364), he would perhaps have attained the eminence as a collector of which his fine portrait now in the Louvre (the oldest extant French portrait) and the illustrations of a Bible translated at his command by Jean de Cis (*circa* 1355) hold out the promise. The Bible was left unfinished, but its all too few completed paintings (Fig. 58) and its remarkable sketches foreshadow the profound changes of the second half of the 14th century (a later artist took up the decoration of the book, but did not finish it; Pl. LXV). We lose sight of Jean Pucelle in the face of a totally different style. Less artificial—and also less elegant and so perhaps less pleasing to the refined taste of the court—it is also more direct, more in the style of the

naturalistic portrait of John the Good. Possibly both Bible and portrait are by Girard d'Orléans, the king's official painter. This kind of art was the choice of the king in person, whereas Pucelle's descendants worked for his courtiers. The two styles existed side by side independently of one another, and they represent, before the great confrontation of European styles of which Paris was soon to be the stage, two fundamental aspects of Parisian art. On the one hand, there was the preciosity—restrained and not unduly refined—which makes every composition by Pucelle and his followers both a marvel of skillfully calculated suppleness and a harmonious piece of decoration, unmatched in Europe at the time (but never more than that, for unlike Romanesque decoration it had been emptied of all spiritual content). Beside this exquisite and perfect art, which was

57 – THE ENTOMBMENT. HOURS OF PARIS USE, CIRCA 1330 (MUSÉE JACQUEMART-ANDRÉ, MS. I, F. 187)

58 – ELEAZER AND REBECCA. BIBLE OF JEAN DE CIS, CIRCA 1355 (BIBLIOTHÈQUE NATIONALE, MS. FR. 15397, F. 40 V.)

none the less ephemeral, lacking in vigour and, so to speak, inbred, stood a new feeling—the sense that life in the world outside the studio lay open, in all its variety, to the curiosity of the painter. Pucelle studied Italian forms, but he saw in them little more than another source of decoration. Girard d'Orleans, if we may use his name collectively for the whole group of the king's painters, seems to have had a better understanding of Italian painting. His paintings do not simply imitate its forms, they embody its spirit. With him decoration gives way to the representation of reality—a reality that was adapted to the world of painting, but then all art transposes. The pictures in the Bible of Jean de Cis and even more the astonishing tinted drawings in a copy of the works of the poet and musician Guillaume de Machaut (*circa* 1370) caused a positive revolution in Paris. Here, for the first time so far as we know, the characters move through a natural and independent landscape, grasped in its totality and no longer merely suggested by summary indications. Man is surrounded by nature in all her disorderly profusion. A meadow stretches away to the horizon (raised high, as it is still subject to the flat plane), full of flowers, of copses (*boqueteaux*) in which perch birds that have flown in from the margins, and of buildings imitated from Italian art but from now on

incorporated in the landscape. The fields are alive with flocks of sheep and with various kinds of small game. Springs and ponds diversify the scene, and a road passes through it, busy with the comings and goings of country folk (Pl. LVI). They are charming scenes, very Parisian in the discreet elegance which, although on another plane, they share with Pucelle's pictures, but in which there is already an element of the storytelling which was gradually to dissociate illumination from the text and eventually to destroy it. The characteristic group of trees has caused the style to be attributed to a "Maître aux Boqueteaux", and the name is convenient and even apt, as long as we realise that it covers a diverse group of artists united by a single tendency (Fig. 59). Illumination was already beginning to alter course, long before the great period of international activity of which 15th-century Paris was the scene.

The humanist taste of the king's painters was in keeping with the king's own humanism. Charles V, the son of John the Good, was interested in history, science and literature, and he formed a library at the Louvre which was well stocked with learned works translated at his orders by Jean Golein, Simon de Hesdin, Raoul de Presles, Jean Corbichon and Denis Foulechat, and decorated by Frenchmen of the Boqueteaux group (Pl. LVII). Moreover, he did

not confine his patronage to French artists. A Bible now at The Hague, copied for him on the instructions of Jean de Vaudetar in 1372, contains an interesting portrait of the sovereign signed by Jean Bondol, otherwise known as Jean de Bruges, who may also have executed the other illustrations in the volume. The artist's name indicates his origin; he was painter to the King from at least 1371 onwards, and he and his assistants also decorated a *Cité de Dieu* for Charles v in 1376. With these works Flanders made its official entry into Paris.

We now enter a period of deepening obscurity. Artists of French origin were forced to compete with rivals who flocked to Paris from every side, drawn thither by cultivated patrons who loved luxury and responded to every new manifestation of art and taste. All is confusion, and the only means by which we can unravel the apparently inextricable tangle is the study of style. A certain number of anonymous "masters" can be isolated without too much difficulty, but with few exceptions their origin cannot be established and we call them after the patron who commissioned their best work. The history of French illumination is now centred round the names of certain great collectors. The principal contribution from outside was from the North of France, from the Low Countries and from the district of the Meuse; after that from Italy and finally, as we shall see, perhaps from Spain. The movement began when Charles v took Jean de Bruges into his service, and his action produced a ground swell which profoundly disturbed Parisian and French traditions throughout the whole reign of Charles vi.

Paris and International Art

The native French artists seem to have organized themselves to resist the newcomers, if we are to interpret thus the statutes which the "peintres et imagiers" of Paris had confirmed by the provost on 12 Aug. 1391. They were quickly surrounded, but not submerged, by the flood, and they succeeded in making one essential contribution, an outlook which they were able to impose on the strangers and which in spite of everything unified their efforts. Art, in all its aspects, pursued an unbroken course and "international Gothic" was still essentially French. In fact the foreigners restored to the France of

Charles vi, in a modified and enriched form, what 13th- and 14th-century France had given to Europe as a whole. Most of the newcomers came from the region between French Hainault and Gelderland. Some are known to have been in the service of certain great collectors. Others, grouped together in workshops, are known only by their anonymous works and we are hard put to distinguish one from another and to detach them from their group, since their styles mixed and blended in a constant

59 – MITHRIDATES MASSACRES THE ROMANS. ST. AUGUSTINE, CITÉ DE DIEU, 1376 (BIBLIOTHÈQUE NATIONALE, MS. FR. 22912, F. 94 V.)

process of exchange and imitation. The demands of mass production led to the adoption of formulas, to the mechanical repetition of attitudes and the kind of mannered overemphasis that exaggerates and yet simplifies the expression of character and emotion. However, their mannerism was agreeable and full of life, and there is no doubt that it was necessary. The old French stock was in danger of withering away, and it required just such a graft of gesticulating animation, movement and bold colouring, with new harmonies of orange, carmine and almond. The new elements were imported, along with certain types

60 – CASSANDRA. BOCCACIO, DES CLAIRES ET NOBLES FEMMES, CIRCA 1403 (BIBLIOTHÈQUE NATIONALE, MS. FR. 598, F. 48 V.)

of features and of modelling, and figures of stocky, solid stature, from the Meuse and Westphalia, where they occur in, for example, the work of Meister Bertram.

This varied but united group has been banded together under the name of the "Peintre de 1402", a personality with as many sides to his character as the Maître aux Boqueteaux. Two pairs of manuscripts executed in this workshop one after the other give a good idea of its style: *Femmes célèbres* of Boccaccio and *Bible historiale* of Des Moulins (Pl. LVIII). One copy of the latter, which was painted in two different stages, shows clearly the transition from the old French tradition to the new style. The painter of the frontispiece has preserved the linear modelling, the unbroken colours, and even the shades of the 14th century, as, for instance, in the hair. But in the second

gathering there is a sudden change; a new and vigorous team of artists has taken over, and their lively drawing, the gestures and attitudes of their figures, and their method of suggesting forms simply by means of a play of light exhibit a new feeling for movement and space. The same group decorated a copy of Boccaccio presented to Jean de Berry in 1404, in which one of the painters has revealed his origin by the three words of Dutch which he has put into the mouth of the prophetess Cassandra (Fig. 60). His fellow artists, who differ in the details of their technique but not in their style, also came from the Low Countries, as did all the other members of this very homogeneous group. Once established at Paris, the workshop of the "Peintre de 1402" became a natural centre for Dutch artists. Its most celebrated members were the Limbourg brothers from Nijmegen, whose connection with the workshop is attested by certain traits of style; possibly it was there that Jean de Berry discovered them in about 1410.

To work for this distinguished and extravagant collector was the summit of every artist's, merchant's and courtier's ambition. He seems to have preferred the artists of the Dutch group and to have had fewer dealings with the rival group lead by the masters whom we call by the names of Bedford, Boucicaut and Rohan: a matter of taste on his part, and also, no doubt, a matter of the shrewd commercial sense of the Dutch artists.

A *Cité de Dieu*, dating from about 1410, provides another good example of the style of the workshops in which the Limbourg brothers served their apprenticeship (Pl. LIX).

Among the foreign artists at Paris, the Italians deserve to occupy a place of honour beside the Mosans. From the end of the 14th century onwards numerous contacts were established between France and Lombardy. The Milanese called in French architects to complete the building of their Cathedral; French romances enjoyed in Northern Italy a vogue which the many manuscripts illustrated by Italian artists attest; and the notes of an Italian connoisseur of painting named Alchiero, between 1382 and 1411, collected by the Parisian registrar Jean Lebègue, another connoisseur, show how important were the exchanges between the two countries. A painter who signed himself Zebo da Firenze illustrated a Book of Hours at Paris, in about 1410, for Charles the

Noble, King of Navarre of the Évreux branch: its borders are adorned with flowers and mantling of the kinds that were to inspire the Limbourg brothers a few years later (Fig. 61). Other Italians, in the circle of Christine de Pisan, who was herself of Italian origin, illustrated under her direction certain of her own writings (Pl. LXI); or perhaps there was only one painter, a Lombard certainly, the direct descendant of Giovannino de' Grassi and, in a sense, the distant precursor of Pisanello. Oddly enough this talented and original painter, imbued with wit and even irony, seems to have worked for nobody but Christine. His paintings, which so far as we know were executed in about 1400–1405, were so advanced by Parisian standards that they must have surprised and even shocked his French colleagues, and his influence, if any, was of a very general nature. His impressionist manner (Fig. 62), his astonishing feeling for colour and the freedom of his imagination have left no direct traces, but they doubtless helped, like the flowers of Zebo da Firenze and his like, and the woodland scenes in copies of the *Tacuinum Sanitatis*, to awaken in the Paris school an appreciation of nature. A few French artists did attempt, not unsuccessfully, to imitate these Italians (Pl. LXII).

The Painters of Jean de Berry

Of the many treasures assembled by Jean, Duc de Berry (d. 1416), the youngest brother of Charles V, we possess only part of his library and some of his inventories. The latter appear so precise as to make it possible to identify with complete accuracy the volumes which he purchased or commissioned. In fact, while the identity of certain manuscripts appears beyond doubt, that of others is less certain.

The Psalter of Bourges use, which dates from about 1380–1385, presents no difficulty. Twenty-four miniatures precede the text, twelve Prophets and twelve Apostles in grisaille, painted as we know by André Beauneveu of Valenciennes. The Prophets declare the truths of the Faith, which the Apostles express in the form of articles of the Creed, the appropriate verse of which is inscribed below each Apostle. In this volume, commissioned by him, Jean de Berry imitated the magnificent 13th-century Psalters decorated with a continuous series of full-page paintings not directly related to the text and forming an independ-

ent cycle. The theme of the concordance between the Old and New Testaments, which was an unchanging and always fertile subject of medieval exegis, gave Beauneveu the chance to execute, in painting, a magnificent series of statues which are worthy of one who was both a great sculptor and a master of the brush (Pl. LXIII). The broad and simple modelling of these high reliefs and the brightness of the eyes, which are the only points of colour in a grisaille relieved by the faintest of washes, contrast with the general softness of the paintings which Jean de Berry had inserted in a Book of Hours now

61 – HELL. HOURS OF CHARLES THE NOBLE, CIRCA 1410 (PRIVATE COLLECTION, F. 211)

59

62 – DAWN. CHRISTINE DE PISAN, L'ÉPÎTRE D'OTHÉA À HECTOR, CIRCA 1400–1402 (BIBLIOTHÈQUE NATIONALE, MS. FR. 606, F. 21 V.)

pieces, he never allowed his harrassed "workmen" the time to finish their tasks. It was given away in 1412 to Robinet d'Étampes, the keeper of the duke's jewels, who divided it into two parts. After many adventures the first part has come to rest in the Bibliothèque Nationale in Paris. The second part was again divided into two sections, of which the first was lost through fire in the University Library at Turin in 1904. This fire destroyed the magnificent paintings added soon after the first partition of the manuscript, in about 1417–1420—paintings of such beauty that some have attributed them to Hubert and Jan van Eyck. The problem of their authorship is insoluble, since only photographs of them remain, although a few miniatures from the same group have survived in the third fragment of the book, which is now in the Museo Civico at Turin (Pl. LXVI). The same artist also executed most of what survives of the *Grandes Heures*, which was finished in 1409, and some of its little figures reproduce the pictures of the *Très belles heures de Notre-Dame* (Pl. LXVII). He was an excellent painter, and the famous grisaille painting in the Louvre known as the *Parement de Narbonne* seems to be another example of his work. His career, which may have begun at the end of Charles V's reign, continued in Jean de Berry's service until about 1410 at the latest. On the evidence of the inventories he has been identified as Jacquemart de Hesdin. A recent comparison has resulted in the identification of a Christ carrying the Cross in the Louvre as one of the 45 "grandes peintures" recorded in the inventory of 1413 as being executed by Jacquemart for the *Grandes heures* and lost since the 16th century or earlier; and also in the attribution to Jacquemart, in agreement with the inventory of 1402, despite certain differences due perhaps to their condition or to their slightly earlier date, of the paintings in the *Très belles heures de Notre-Dame* now at Brussels.

The *Très belles heures* at Brussels bears the traces of numerous modifications. At the beginning, Jean de Berry added a double-page miniature in which he is shewn kneeling, between SS. John and Andrew, before a Virgin with a Petition. It is a beautiful piece of painting but one which hardly justifies the unreserved admiration which is generally accorded to it (Fig. 63). Its style is feeble and it is marred by shocking lapses into clumsiness, which can be explained if, as seems likely, it was copied in the form of a

at Brussels and which, in spite of all appearances, have been attributed to Beauneveu.

At the same time as Beauneveu, Jean de Berry had in his service a distinguished anonymous painter to whom he entrusted part of the decoration of the *Petites Heures*, which seems to date from 1390. It is in fact not certain that the volume was executed for the duke himself, although the Office of St. John is elaborated in a significant fashion; but it is at any rate worthy of the great collector (Pl. LXIV). A little later, perhaps about 1405–1407, the same artist decorated most of the *Très belles heures de Notre-Dame*. Like many of Jean de Berry's books it remains unfinished; always impatient to possess new master-

63 – VIRGIN AND CHILD. TRÈS BELLES HEURES DE NOTRE-DAME, CIRCA 1409 (BRUSSELS, BIBLIOTHÈQUE ROYALE, MS. 11060-61, F. 11)

64 – VIRGIN AND CHILD. COLLECTION OF DEVOTIONAL TREATISES, 1406 (BIBLIOTHÈQUE NATIONALE, MS. FR. 926, F. 2)

diptych from another Virgin with a Petition, frontispiece to a collection of pious treatises presented to Marie de Berry, the duke's daughter, by her confessor Simon de Courcy in 1406. I attribute the latter to Pol de Limbourg, before he entered the household of Jean de Berry (Fig. 64). The theme of the Virgin with a Petition, new at that date, was to achieve a certain success in later years; it certainly seems to have caught the duke's fancy, for he immediately had it copied by one of his own painters. Jacquemart de Hesdin disappeared about 1409 at the latest. To replace him the duke called in three young artists, nephews of Jean Malouel, painter to Philip the Bold, Duke of Burgundy. Their home was in Gelderland and they had come to complete their training at Paris. On 6 March 1402 Philip had taken the two elder brothers, Pol and Jean, into his employment and acquired the exclusive right to their services for four years; but on 24 April 1404 he died, and everything points to the two brothers, joined now by their youngest brother, Hermann,

having then worked in some Mosan workshop at Paris, together with other Dutch artists. From this Parisian period date two miniatures which we may fairly ascribe to one of them, presumably Pol. Both miniatures possess the qualities which the brothers developed so wonderfully in later years, and their subjects were repeated exactly in books which they decorated for Jean de Berry soon afterwards. One, a Court of Heaven, decorates a *Légende dorée* whose text was completed in 1404; it is reproduced detail for detail in the *Belles Heures* (Fig. 65). The other is closely connected with Jean de Berry: the Virgin with a Petition of 1406, already mentioned, which he had copied in the *Très belles heures de Notre-Dame* now at Brussels. In 1406 the Limbourgs had not yet entered the duke's household and Jacquemart de Hesdin may already have disappeared from view: so it was another painter, one of his "workmen" as they

65 – THE COURT OF HEAVEN. LÉGENDE DORÉE, 1404 (BIBLIO-
THÈQUE NATIONALE, MS. FR. 414, F. 1)

onseigneur sait
Jerosime dit ce
ste auttorite sar
tousiours rien
ne chose de bien que le deable ne te
tentne ose seulz Et monseignin e
augustin dit ou liure de leuure des moi
nes que nul home puissant delabou
rer ne soit estre oyseulz Pour la
quelle chose quant je eux parfait et

rcompli le miner des hystoire du
monde. Et translate du latin en fran
cois a la requeste de tres puissant et
noble dame madame jehanne de bou
rgoigne Royne de fra̅ce par la gr̅ace
de dieu je fus tout esbahi a quelle oeu
ure faire je me meetroie apres si trés
haulte et longue oeuure come je auo
re fait par deuant …

were called, a conscientious artist but no genius, old-fashioned in spite of his talent (which is why he is dated too early), who was ordered to copy their Virgin with a Petition. Such at least is the reconstruction which a study of the work suggests. Like many another exacting patron, Jean de Berry brought out latent powers in the young Limbourgs and his influence perfected the qualities which they owed to their Mosan ancestry and their Parisian training. In his milieu they became familiar with the teaching of Italy, which could be found everywhere in the collections of their new master. In contact with the rarest and most exquisite products of all the arts of Europe their impetuous genius rose to superb heights.

First came the *Belles Heures*, *c.* 1410–13 (Pl. LXVIII), in which Pol—the eldest of the brothers and their leader—achieved a brilliant synthesis of all the various tendencies and borrowings of the international Gothic of Paris. Restraint, a slightly cold but smiling elegance, a discreet avoidance of excess, a kind of peaceful charm—all inherited from the best French tradition, from the Psalter of St. Louis to Jean Pucelle; Mosan colouring and a taste for movement which bordered on mannerism and in the workshop of the "Peintre de 1402" became a mechanical device; a feeling, derived from Italy, for volume and depth which was to complete the conquest of sensible appearances, of nature, and of the humanism of which there are already signs in French literature and learning—such are its chief characteristics. The *Belles Heures* is a major work; it marks, about 1413, the end of one epoch and the beginning of another, and is the link between the two. It was a triumph for the Limbourg brothers, but also for Jean de Berry who had brought out the best in them, and for Paris which had trained them and fed their genius on the riches of all Europe. The climax of medieval illumination, it marks also its conclusion. Illumination now breaks away from the flat surface to which it had hitherto been confined; the vertical plane is tilted backwards; the horizon drops to eye-level and reveals the sky, empty space and infinity.

The *Belles Heures* contains the earliest example in French painting of an organic landscape: stormy sky and raging sea (Fig. 66). Until then no painter of French extraction had ever attempted such a subject; nor, except for Pol de Limbourg himself in the *Très riches heures*, which he painted for Jean de Berry

66 – MIRACLE OF ST. NICHOLAS. BELLES HEURES DE JEAN DE BERRY, BETWEEN 1410 AND 1413 (NEW YORK, CLOISTERS MUSEUM, F. 168)

a few years later, was any artist to attempt its like until the time of Fouquet and Jean Colombe. And yet ten years earlier the painter of Christine de Pisan had dared such a theme; his efforts, unprecedented in illumination and without any immediate following, may explain the sudden appearance of landscape in the work of the Limbourgs. Other signs connect them with Lombardy: the circular capital surmounted by a "tabernacle" with figures imitated from the pillars (before 1390) of Milan Cathedral, the mantling derived from acanthus leaves and used to form medallions, and many other small but significant details, quite apart from the general characteristics indicated above. There is, however, no need to suppose that the Limbourgs travelled in Italy; Jean de Berry's immense collections are in themselves a sufficient explanation.

67 – THE KILL. TRÈS RICHES HEURES DE JEAN DE BERRY, 1416 (CHANTILLY, MUSÉE CONDÉ, MS. 65, F. 12 V.)

68 – HELL. TRÈS RICHES HEURES DE JEAN DE BERRY, 1416 (CHANTILLY, MUSÉE CONDÉ, MS. 65, F. 108)

Perhaps at about the same time the three brothers began work on the illustration of a *Bible historiée*. Each completed only a single gathering, abandoning the rest to other later artists, whose work steadily deteriorates, until about 1475, and is eventually left unfinished (Pl. LXIX). This interruption bears all the marks of Jean de Berry's nervous unrest; his plans were always being disturbed by new projects, by his greedy, interfering nature; but we cannot be sure that the Bible was in fact commissioned by him. A mere fragment, scarcely begun, it appears in none of his inventories and contains no mark of his ownership. In addition to a portrait of the duke added to the *Petites Heures* (Pl. LXX), there are two other strangely heavy paintings by the Limbourgs in the *Très belles heures de Notre-Dame*, which, in all honesty, are quite unworthy of them.

Their greatest masterpiece was interrupted by the unknown accident which carried them off in February or March 1416, four months before the death of Jean de Berry. In the inventory drawn up after his death it aptly is described as the *Très riches heures*. In 1855 it was acquired by the Duc d'Aumale, who bequeathed it to the Institut de France as part of his incomparable library. It is a perfect example of what can be obtained, from artists who are in any case more than ordinarily gifted, by the exacting will of a connoisseur. Jean de Berry's instructions certainly counted for much in the execution of this justly famous volume which is not only the Limbourgs' greatest work but the masterpiece of medieval illumination. The well-known scenes of the kalendar, one for each of the twelve months of the year, are not laid, as in other Books of Hours, in a neutral and anonymous setting, but in the duke's own milieu: at his lavish and hospitable table, among the members

69 – ALEXANDER AT TABLE. BIBLE HISTORIALE, CIRCA 1420
(CHANTILLY, MUSÉE CONDÉ, MS. 28, F. 24 V.)

70 – THE NATIVITY. HCURS OF PARIS USE, CIRCA 1415 (COL-
LECTION OF COUNT ANTOINE SEILERN, F. 34 V.)

of his household, on his estates, at the gates of his magnificent châteaux, or in Paris, before the Cité and the Louvre, which the duke could see from his town house, the Hôtel de Nesles. But although the traditional scenes are laid in everyday settings, which are exact imitations of actual places, they belong to an ideal world, full of grace, luxury and the charm of pastoral poetry. Realism has given rein to the imagination (Fig. 67).

The Limbourgs were exact observers of landscape and they found mysterious correspondences between the forms of nature and the landscapes of the mind. Far from breaking down appearances to uncover the realities which they conceal, after the manner of the Romanesque painters, they looked into them and found in their secret harmony the signs of a higher order. Three superb pictures in the *Très riches heures* distil the essence of their genius, which was capable both of minute fidelity to nature and of synthesis: the Fall of the rebel Angels, Hell (Fig. 68), and the Coronation of the Virgin. We may consider the last (Pl. LXXI). The picture, rounded in its lower register into a double curve, tapers as it rises and dissolves into golds and azures, like a cloud evaporating in the light and warmth of heaven. Everything unites in this ascension to glorify the exaltation of the Virgin, but the idea is expressed in symbols which are in no way stylized or abstract.

The loss, at the height of their powers, of these painters who seemed destined to alter the whole course of painting, accounts for the paucity of their influence on French illumination. Nobody attempted to imitate them, except to copy a few of their themes (Fig. 69); and it seems certain that the beautiful Book of Hours now in the possession of Count Antoine Seilern, in London (Fig. 70), is by a Lim-

66

bourg, perhaps the brother who painted the first gathering of the *Bible historiée*, who is also the author of a work in the Musée Condé (Fig. 71). The Seilern Hours is in many respects a replica of the *Belles Heures*, and its borders and certain of its compositions foreshadow the *Très riches heures* at Chantilly. It cannot be later than 1416 or earlier than 1413, and it was left unfinished, to be completed later by a Flemish artist. It seems to be missing from the posthumous inventory, and although it was probably executed at the duke's court, there is nothing to show that it was made for him.

For the duke, who was so fond of receiving presents, was himself generous. He gave to Etienne Loypeau, archbishop of Luçon, his protégé, a Pontifical, and to the Sainte-Chapelle, Bourges, founded in 1404, a Lectionary and a Gospel-book—all decorated by "workmen" of his about whom we know nothing else. We are equally in the dark about the excellent artist who began for Jean de Berry the *Antiquités judaïques* which was completed in about 1470 by Fouquet. He cannot have been in the duke's service for long, and he seems to have been taken on trial, some time about 1410, between the death of Jacquemart de Hesdin and the arrival of the Limbourg brothers (Pl. LX).

The Bedford, Boucicaut and Rohan Masters, and their Group

Complete obscurity envelops the life of the painter whom we call the Maître de Bedford, after John of Lancaster, Duke of Bedford, regent of France for the King of England after the treaty of Troyes, and the recipient of two important works painted between 1424 and 1435 for himself and his wife: a Breviary in Paris (Pl. LXXII) and a Book of Hours in London. A prolific artist, the Maître de Bedford began his career about 1405 and was active until after 1430. During this long period he collaborated with several different artists, one of whom, the Maître de Boucicaut, seems to have remained in his circle to the end, while another, the Maître de Rohan, left him in about 1414 to enter the service of the house of Anjou. The three were only loosely associated, since each worked also on his own and with other less talented illuminators at various stages in his career. The group is quite distinct from the Mosan work-

shops at Paris, which we referred to collectively as the "Peintre de 1402"; yet none of its members possess characteristics which are sharply enough defined to point to a particular origin, whether in France or abroad. Grouped together, they retained the individuality which they owed to their different temperaments and trainings, although certain common technical and decorative devices indicate that they made the sort of artistic exchanges natural among collaborators. Of the three, Bedford was the most active and the most open to new ideas: a true painter and colourist, he never resorted to the pen to sharpen his contours or his modelling; his colours are hazy, as if bathed in a soft and harmonious light, which enhances the roundness of features and faces and the suppleness of draperies, but he took little interest in expressions or attitudes. To begin with his compositions were traditional (Fig. 72), but he gradually introduced into his pictures realistic land-

71 — THE PRESENTATION IN THE TEMPLE. HOURS OF PARIS USE, CIRCA 1410–1415 (CHANTILLY, MUSÉE CONDÉ, MS. 66, F. 69)

67

72 – THE NATIVITY. BEDFORD BREVIARY, BETWEEN 1424 AND 1435 (BIBLIOTHÈQUE NATIONALE, MS. LAT. 17294, F. 56 V.)

certainty on these points. Bedford's outstanding gifts as a colourist and his preference for many-coloured landscapes reappear in a copy of the *Livre de la chasse* by Gaston de Foix (Pl. LXXIV). The changing landscapes, the woods and the fields under cultivation, each so different, in which large and small animals disport themselves—all observed with the eye of an expert—place the Bedford Master in the front rank of outdoor painters. And yet his work does not approach the landscapes of the Limbourgs: no breath of air enlivens his faithful and sensitive pictures, which are chiefly remarkable for their dexterity. Another example of his dexterity is the delightful Coëtivy Hours, painted some years later in various shades of white.

73 – THE ANNUNCIATION TO THE SHEPHERDS. HOURS OF THE MARÉCHAL DE BOUCICAUT, CIRCA 1410–1415 (MUSÉE JACQUE-MART-ANDRÉ, MS. 2, F. 79)

scapes in the Italian style, peopled with lively crowds arranged so as to suit a perspective that was only just beginning to be tilted down towards the horizon. His masterpieces, the Bedford Breviary and the Bedford Hours, are a mass of picturesque and varied scenes, even in the borders, which he was the first to make an integral part of the illustration of the whole page, completing the central scene.

The admirable *Térence des ducs* in the Bibliothèque de l'Arsenal (Pl. LXXIII)—so called after the Dauphin Louis of Guyenne and Jean de Berry, to whom it belonged—was evidently decorated by three painters between 1405 and 1410. One of them was doubtless the Maître de Bedford, whose exquisite feeling for colour may be recognised in its bold harmonies, and the other two were probably members of his workshop; but it is difficult to speak with

His closest collaborator, whom we call the Maître de Boucicaut, after a handsome Book of Hours (Fig. 73) which he executed in about 1410–1415 for Jean Le Meingre, Maréchal de Boucicaut, joined with him in the decoration of two manuscripts. The first is the celebrated *Livre des Merveilles* (Pl. LXXV), a collection of the Eastern travels of Marco Polo and others in the 13th and 14th centuries that received this name at the beginning of the 15th. The second is a rather later Breviary of Paris use, now at Châteauroux, of which the summer section—all that survives— bears the arms of a Dauphin who is possibly the future Charles VII (Fig. 74). Boucicaut is hard to distinguish from Bedford, except that his style is less exclusively pictorial (Pl. LXXVI). He used line to sharpen his modelling; his work was more elegant but also drier (Fig. 75), less atmospheric; and he was not afraid to use raw, even acid colours. He was especially good at interiors and knew how to people them with figures; he had an instinctive feeling for linear perspective; and his pure, calm, rather cold style diverged in this respect, despite the close links which at times confound them, from that of Bedford and to an even greater degree from that of the third member of this Parisian group, the so-called Maître de Rohan.

Yolanda of Aragon, wife of Louis II, Duke of Anjou and King of Sicily, daughter of John I and niece of Martin the Aged (both book-lovers), purchased at the posthumous sale of Jean de Berry's library one of its finest volumes, the *Belles Heures*. She suggested it to her official painter as a model and he copied certain scenes to illustrate a book intended for one of Yolanda's sons, perhaps the future King Louis. This work, executed in about 1418–1425, is the famous *Heures de Rohan*, so called after the armorial bearings which were added later. Before entering Yolanda's service, the painter had collaborated with the Bedford group in the production of popular works such as Froissart's *Chronicle*, the *Bible historiale* of Guiart des Moulins, and treatises on hunting like the *Livre du roi Modus et de la reine Ratio* and Gaston de Foix, and later had specialised in Books of Hours of medium quality (Fig. 76). Like Jean de Berry with the Limbourg brothers, the Queen of Sicily lifted the Maître de Rohan out of his commercial rut. In her circle he was able to engage assistants and establish a workshop, from which she commissioned not only the volume from which the

74 – THE MARTYRDOM OF ST. DIONYSIUS. PARIS BREVIARY, CIRCA 1420 (CHÂTEAUROUX, MS. 2, F. 364)

master takes his name but two other Books of Hours, probably intended for her second son René and her daughter Yolanda. The workshop later decorated a fourth book, of the use of Angers, which is called the Martin Le Roy Hours after a recent owner; we cannot say whether it was made for a member of the House of Anjou.

Though he came from the Bedford-Boucicaut workshop, the Rohan master far surpasses his old associates. The pathos which permeates his work sets him apart from his contemporaries. Whereas they based their style on technical innovations, intoxicated by the discovery of life, of nature and of man, he ignored the discovery of volume and shunned the picturesque. His scenes are placed against a diapered background and have a strictly vertical perspective, as if nothing had changed since the time of Charles V; architectural features are either neglected or incoherent. Among French illuminators his style is unique. His human figures are stockily-built and heavy, as if oppressed by a destiny which eludes their comprehension; there is a look of anxiety in their veiled eyes; their flesh

75 – THE ANNUNCIATION. HOURS OF PARIS USE, CIRCA 1410–1415 (BIBLIOTHÈQUE MAZARINE, MS. 469, F. 13)

is grey or an orange red. Divine personages are slight and pale, their expressions powerful and serene, and they are painted with the utmost reverence. The artist of Yolanda's choice may perhaps have come, like her, from Aragon: a Spanish lady would naturally have been interested in a painter from her own country, just as Christine de Pisan had been interested in the Lombard painters resident in Paris; and if we look for illuminators whose style we may compare with his we find them not in Paris but in Languedoc and Catalonia (Fig. 77).

Whatever his origin, his contribution to Parisian and French art was unique. An obsession with death and the after-life everywhere haunts the great paintings of the *Heures de Rohan:* the Descent from the Cross and the Dead Man face to face with his Judge (Pl. LXXVII). The painter dwells on the dead man's shrunken and bloodless corpse, its paleness emphasised by the dark cloth on which it lies; the

bones scattered round it on the ground symbolize the mournful dissolution that awaits it. The man's soul escapes with difficulty from the devil who disputes its possession with the Archangel Raphael, but God bends forward to receive it in a blaze of compassion. In the kalendar peasants perform with patient resignation the tasks of which the signs of the Zodiac, menacing and huge, mark the inexorable return. Here is nothing to recall the lighthearted recklessness that was everywhere the vogue, the fever of artistic discovery, the luxury and the elegance, which contrasted so strangely with the political crisis and the military disasters that had cast their shadow over an heroic but impetuous nobility and with it almost the whole of France. The anguish in the painter's heart moves us as deeply as the accents of a Villon. The latest works in which the Maître de Rohan took any part seem to date from about 1430, and after the end of his long career his assistants and the pupils whom he had trained continued, in the West and in Britany, to produce books in the same style; but their work is insipid and retains none of the genius of their master.

The primacy of Paris came to an end in about 1420, soon after the death of Jean de Berry, when the Treaty of Troyes placed the North of France, along with the capital, under the dominion of the King of England. Charles VI died in 1422, leaving his throne and a gravely disordered nation to a young man aged only nineteen. French illumination entered a period of confusion in which the brilliant artists of the international period were followed by men of straw. A single painter stands out from the crowd of indecisive talents, the assured and witty illustrator of a Book of Hours made for Margaret of Orleans, who in 1426 married Richard, Count of Étampes, the son of John V of Montfort, Duke of Britany (Pl. LXXVIII). His lively compositions, with their bright colours, are a little hard, but nothing can equal the fantasy of his borders, which are designed with the utmost boldness and skill. They contain either hunting-scenes, cavalcades and groups of travellers moving through forests whose trees are gigantic flowers, or else a scattering of various small objects forming a simple abstract pattern. These marginal decorations and certain details of style suggest that he was connected with the Maître de Bedford, and the same general style recurs, down to about 1470, in a Book of Hours of Rouen use; in several

76 – THE ANNUNCIATION. HOURS OF TROYES USE, CIRCA 1410–1415 (CHANTILLY, MUSÉE CONDÉ, MS. 77, F. 29)

77 – THE CRUCIFIXION. ROMAN MISSAL, SECOND HALF OF THE 14TH CENTURY (CAMBRAI, MS. 150, F. 176)

copies of the chronicle of Jean de Courcy, Seigneur de Bourg-Achard, which is known as *La Bouquechardière*; and in a Valerius Maximus and a Guillaume de Tyr both from the Échevinage of Rouen (Fig. 78). The evidence suggests that a group of artists was formed in Normandy round John of Lancaster (d. 1435), who resided at Rouen, and that they were active over a period of many years. Paris was losing its power and official art moved away to the new political centre of the kingdom. From the middle to the end of the 15th century the Loire valley and the new capitals at Tours and Bourges usurped the position of Paris. In the North, the powerful state of Philip the Good absorbed the vital energies of painting and produced magnificent schools formed of both French and Flemish elements. They were not strictly speaking French, but their brilliance was soon to acquire an unrivalled fascination for the last generation of French illuminators.

Jean Fouquet

At the end of a copy of the *Antiquités judaïques* which belonged to Louis XI's son-in-law Pierre de Beaujeu, the latter's secretary, François Robertet, wrote: "In this book are twelve miniatures, the first three by the illuminator of Jean, Duc de Berry, the other nine by the good painter and illuminator of Louis XI, Jean Fouquet, a native of Tours." Without this unique piece of evidence the greatest French painter of the 15th century would remain, like so many others, an enigma. With the help of Robertet's note and the *Antiquités* we are able to attribute a number of works to Fouquet, both miniatures and panel-paintings, some of which are unquestionably his; the authorship of others is less certain. He was admired and imitated; he worked with collaborators and trained pupils; and it is far from easy, at this distance in time, to sort out what he painted with his own hand

71

78 – FULK OF ANJOU MARRIES QUEEN MELISSENDA. GUILLAUME DE TYR, HISTOIRE DE LA CONQUÊTE DE JÉRUSALEM, CIRCA 1460 (BIBLIOTHÈQUE NATIONALE, MS. FR. 2629, F. 167)

in the course of a long career, what he merely designed for his assistants, and what his imitators and pupils executed on their own. We pass imperceptibly from the certain to the doubtful without being able to draw a sharp distinction between the two. Certainly Fouquet developed and varied his style; but who is to say how much?

He was born at Tours in about 1420 and died there between 1477 and 1481. Between 1443 and 1447 he visited Rome and was already well enough known for Eugenius IV to commission his portrait from him. We do not know what he derived from his stay in Rome, since no earlier work has survived, but we may fairly attribute to Italian influence his obvious interest in problems of perspective, which he reveals in his fondness for processions. He usually catches them as they turn a corner, so as to show the figures from different angles; and he portrays buildings in three-quarters profile or full face without hesitating to exaggerate the lines of the perspective, which do not however converge on a vanishing point as they ought. More than any of his French predecessors, not excluding the Limbourg brothers, Fouquet had a feeling for atmosphere. His scenes are bathed in a misty glow which softens their contours and irradiates the distances, giving to his calm and balanced compositions a unity and depth which was equalled only in the final period of the art (Pl. LXXIX). Illumination, in fact, ends with Fouquet, at the moment when Gothic book-decoration had reached its peak. It now deserted the plane surface and evolved into a branch of panel-painting.

At the beginning of the 15th century Jean de Berry commissioned a two-volume *Antiquités judaïques*, but his artist completed only the first three miniatures; in about 1470 James of Armagnac, Duke of Nemours, appointed Fouquet to complete the work and Volume I subsequently fell into the hands of Pierre de Beaujeu; it was thus that Robertet came to add his revealing sentence at the end. The miniatures in Volume II may not all be by Fouquet himself, but they are from his own workshop. The same is true of a copy of Boccaccio's *Cas des nobles hommes et femmes*, now at Munich, which was copied in 1458 and decorated for Laurent Girard, the comptroller general of receipt; Fouquet himself certainly painted the superb frontispiece (Fig. 79). Famous in his lifetime, and at an early age, and painter to the King, Fouquet had, like other artists of the period, to undertake

79 – THE PARLIAMENT OF VENDÔME. BOCCACCIO, DES CAS DES NOBLES HOMMES ET FEMMES, 1458 (MUNICH, BAYERISCHE STAATSBIBLIOTHEK, COD. GALL. 6, F. 2 V.)

all kinds of work, from the painting of portraits to the preparation of royal processions. There are many traces in the written records of the time of Fouquet himself, his family and his works. The documents provide biographical details and particulars of commissions of which no traces survive, but as far as his work is concerned they have contributed mainly hypotheses and provisional truths, which are better ignored if we are to confine ourselves to what is probable.

Surrounded by assistants and pupils, who doubtless completed works that he had prepared and whose exact contribution it is impossible to assess, Fouquet remains a nebula. So, for the same reasons, do Colombe, Bourdichon and the other successful artists of the period; but Fouquet's case is the most important and the most vexing. We recognise in him the

most accomplished exponent of French illumination at its height, at the moment when, largely through his influence, it was merging with the autonomous art of panel painting. We should like to draw a sharp line round his commanding figure, but we must be content simply to devine his presence at the centre of a group, of a workshop whose outlines are all too vague.

Confining ourselves to illumination, the first volume of the *Antiquités judaïques*, authenticated by Robertet, is undoubtedly by Fouquet; the Hours of Étienne Chevalier in their entirety, most of the *Grandes Chroniques de France* (and the preparatory stage of the whole work), and the frontispiece of the Munich Boccaccio are almost as certainly his own work. From this evidence we can form an accurate enough

picture of the artist to place him exactly and appreciate his true stature.

Fouquet is thought to have received his training at Paris, for although he was born and lived at Tours, the buildings and landscapes of the capital are so frequently and faithfully portrayed in his pictures that he must have stayed there for long periods and known it very well; but we look in vain for any reflection in his work of the Paris painters of Charles VI's time or of the brilliant set of international artists. By the time Fouquet was born Paris, the artistic centre of France since the 13th century, had lost her dominant position, and her great artists had either vanished or followed their patrons elsewhere—the result of a series of events which took place round about the year 1420. Jean de Berry had died in 1416, shortly

after the Limbourg brothers. In 1419 the Duke of Burgundy, John the Fearless, was assassinated. His son Philip deserted Dijon, Paris and France for Lille and then Brussels, and there grew up round his court a Flemish school of painting which was soon to attract the attention of all Europe. Charles VI had long been a nonentity and when in 1424 his son, a minor, succeeded him it was as "King of Bourges", in accordance with the Treaty of Troyes in 1420. Yet Charles was still King, and Bourges, the old capital city of Jean de Berry, was later to see a period of activity, with Jean Colombe and the group of Central French painters, which can only be explained by the unequal patronage of the duke and the king, or at least by their presence in the city. The Bedford workshop may have moved to Rouen, and the Rohan workshop was established at Angers at the court of Yolanda of Aragon and her son René, who was to provide a focus for a numerous group of artists in Anjou and Provence alike.

Where then did Fouquet study up to the age of about twenty-five, before settling in Tours as a married man and a householder, in 1448 at the latest, and painting Eugenius IV's portrait at Rome (the Pope died in February 1447)? Little time remains for an apprenticeship at Paris, which had in any case lost all its old importance, or elsewhere in France; and if he had such an apprenticeship it has left no traces in his work. The only information that we possess about the young Fouquet is of Italian origin. Gifted as he was (which is what really matters), entirely independent and French as he appears, his early work links him to Italy. Recollections of Italy, still fresh in his mind, abound in the famous Book of Hours which he painted soon after his return, in about 1450, for Étienne Chevalier, and they lie nearer the surface in that volume than in any other part of his work (Pl. LXXX). From Italy, where he had gone, as the son of a priest and a married woman, to seek a pardon for his illegitimacy, Fouquet brought back the science of perspective, which he learnt from his friend Filarete. He was the first to introduce perspective into France and he studied it with obvious pleasure throughout his career, although he was later to handle it in a somewhat unorthodox fashion. He also introduced into his work architectural decorations typical of the early Italian Renaissance: columns and entablatures of classical inspiration, faced with coloured

82 – AN ANGEL AT PRAYER. HOURS OF DIANE DE CROY, CIRCA 1465 (SHEFFIELD, RUSKIN MUSEUM, F. 12 V.)

marbles; gardens and paved courts flanked by walls behind which rise cypresses or hills; and above all, besides the actual forms, a clear and spacious composition and a calm mastery of attitudes and faces, which rarely express strong emotion although they are varied enough and include a number of portraits. Fouquet's Italy was the calm, serene land of Fra Angelico and Piero della Francesca (Fig. 81). Gone are the courtly, rather mannered elegance and the winged fantasy of the Limbourgs and the pathos of the Maître de Rohan, the two extremes of the international art of Paris. Nor should we look for Fouquet's antecedents among lesser artists like the Bedford and Boucicaut Masters, unless in order to draw attention to the gulf that separates them from him. With Fouquet we find ourselves in another world—colder, nobler and more human—and he leads us out of the Middle Ages into the Renaissance. Here this study might end, were it not that the Middle Ages continued, openly or in concealment, until well on into the 16th century.

A taste for reality, exact representation, accurate detail and portraiture—all these are already present in the work of the Limbourgs, but only as the means out of which to create a work of the imagination. For Fouquet they are the end; he goes no further, leaving us at liberty either to remain in this natural world, refined by his care, set in order, purged of the uglinesses which disfigure it and pervert its true nature, or to imagine at leisure what he himself does not even hint at. That is why he attaches such importance to faithful representation and to local colour—or what he took to be local colour. He gathers his facts like a history painter and his scenes are laid in settings which are either real or borrowed from life. In the *Grandes Chroniques de France*, executed in about 1458, perhaps for Charles VII (Pl. LXXXI), Montmartre in the days of Dagobert appears against a panorama of Paris which contains everything that Fouquet was himself able to see from the top of the hill; Charlemagne is crowned in St. Peter's at Rome, and the view of the ancient basilica's interior is one of the best sources we possess for the nature of the building replaced by Bramante; Philip Augustus captures the city of Tours, which is dominated by a minutely faithful representation of the abbey church of Saint-Martin; and it has justly been remarked that Fouquet's series of panoramas and detailed views of Paris are a valuable source of information on the topography of the capital between 1450 and 1470. Certain scenes in the Hours of Étienne Chevalier are pre-sented on a trestle stage, like the scenes in mystery plays; the stage forms a pedestal in front of which are figures which complete or introduce the main scene. Below the Christ before Pilate carpenters are at work on the Cross and one of the thieves is released from prison (Fig. 80); beneath the Christ carrying the Cross a blacksmith and his wife forge the spear and the nails. The theatre reduces life to its essentials, simplifies it and removes, for our benefit, the impurities which obscure its meaning; so do Fouquet's pictures—carefully planned stage settings in which the artist first breaks down reality and then reassembles it so as to bring out its true character.

Fouquet was the King's painter and his brilliance permeated not only his immediate circle but practically the whole of French painting in the second half of the 15th century. The centre of artistic activity was from now on the valley of the Loire, between Angers, which was King René's capital, and Bourges, where Jean Colombe worked, including Tours, which was the home of Bourdichon. The accounts and inventories are full of the names of artists, but they tell us nothing, as it is impossible to relate them to the mass of anonymous and approximately dated works of art that have survived. An excellent assistant collaborated closely with Fouquet on the Boccaccio, but we cannot, until we know more, ascribe to him any other works; another had a share in Volume II of the *Antiquités judaïques*; and several Books of Hours painted between 1460 and 1470 bear indubitable signs of the master's hand. The Hours of Anne de Beaujeu, formerly in the Paul Durrieu collection, also contains little miniatures by the François who is believed to have been Fouquet's son (we shall return to him) and a remarkable bust of Christ which is very close in style to the portrait in enamel, now in the Louvre, of Fouquet himself. Are the Christ and the portrait by Fouquet's own hand? We may reasonably wonder, if we compare them—and the comparison is not damaging—with the excellent portrait of Louis de Laval by Jean Colombe.

Another painter who is, it seems, to be distinguished from Fouquet is the author of the Hours of Diane de Croy, in the Ruskin Museum, Sheffield (Fig. 82), and of other small volumes; but a detailed analysis of his work remains to be made, and its results will in any case be no more than approximately conclusive. The best criterion, difficult though it is to apply, is the

The text within the illustration reads (left column):

aſſauoir ſe de puis noe Juſques a abialã
len treuue aucunes gens qui aient
veſtu ſelon dieu
...te choſe eſt aſſauoir cierement
par la parole des eſcriptures ſe
les apparances du coure dela ſie
...ite ſoient continuees apres le
deluge ou ſe elles furent entre
...

Jeune de lainſne et greigneur du derreiner
lequel auoit pedue enſon pere et le mauldit
nonne en li maio ou filz dicelu en diſant auſi
mauldit ſoit chanaani lenfant il ſera ſubiet
aſes freres Touteuoiez chanaain auoit eſte
engendre de cham lequel dun mauoit me
couuerte la nudie... deſon pere qui dormoit
amdoie lauoit deſcouuerte dont auſi noeli
noe adiouſta amos la benediction de ſes deux

84 – THE TOWER OF BABEL. ST. AUGUSTINE, CITÉ DE DIEU, CIRCA 1473 (BIBLIOTHÈQUE NATIONALE, MS. FR. 19, F. 81 V.)

influence of Flanders, which is more apparent in some pseudo-Fouquets than in others, while in the real Fouquet it appears rarely or not at all.

The Maître de Jouvenel des Ursins

Among the pseudo-Fouquets there is one artist in whom the Flemish strain is so prominent as to suggest that he was a Fleming who settled in the Loire district towards the middle of the century. He deserves to be rescued from the neglect which has so far been his lot. He has long suffered from being confused with Fouquet, the young Fouquet of the years before his Italian travels, who has so far been sought in vain and who may never have existed. But all the evidence is against this fusion of two such different temperaments, and the dates in any case disallow it. For want of a better name I have called

77

this artist the "Maître de Jouvenel des Ursins", after his most striking work, a copy of the *Mer des histoires* of Giovanni Colonna, painted in 1448–1449 for Guillaume Jouvenel (1401–1472), Chancellor of France. Of his other works the best are perhaps to be found in a *Secrets de l'histoire naturelle* in the Charnacé collection (Fig. 83); in a little Book of Hours of Roman use in the Rothschild collection (Pl. LXXXII); and in a collection of the *Ordonnances* of Charles VII dated to the end of the year 1457. Colours are bathed in a dominant and characteristic golden glow; the faces, which are modelled on the surface by means of flat planes and not, as with Fouquet, in volume, have certain Flemish affinities which we find also in the portrait of the Man with a Glass of Wine in the Louvre: heavy eyes, fleshy nose, fat ears. For my part I have no hesitation in attributing the Man with a Glass of Wine to the Maître de Jouvenel.

Close to this painter, and in the Tours-Angers-Nantes region, secondary artists were at work who form a link with the circle of René of Anjou. Unfortunately we know nothing about them, and apart from René himself, whom the recent researches of Otto Pächt tend to reveal as a painter in his own right, as contemporary sources suggest, the circle has not received the attention it deserves. Broadly speaking, the second half and the end of the 15th century, with which this study ends, are divided between René of Anjou and the direct heirs of Fouquet, Jean Colombe and Jean Bourdichon, followed by the so-called "Rouen" school, in which the pupils of the latter united to achieve a kind of final triumph.

Minor Painters of the End of the 15th Century

Younger than the Maître de Jouvenel, and much further from Fouquet in style, although there is evidence to suggest that he was Fouquet's son, is Maître François. He has left an important series of works and deserves credit for his high professional standards. But François Fouquet (supposing that is his name) inherited nothing from his father. His work is hard, rather vulgar, and monotonous, although his technical dexterity and consistency won him a considerable reputation. Besides a *Cité de Dieu* painted for the King's counsellor Charles de Gaucourt (Fig. 84), he supplied books to Charles VIII, Louis XII and

85 – THE WOMEN OF ISRAEL ACCLAIM DAVID. HOURS OF LOUIS OF SAVOY, BETWEEN 1440 AND 1465 (BIBLIOTHÈQUE NATIONALE, MS. LAT. 9473, F. 76 V.)

Anne of Britany. As skilful in the handling of large crowds as in the minutest details, he was a decorator pure and simple, knowing nothing about atmosphere and the problems it presented to his contemporaries. In the company of Fouquet and René of Anjou he deserves no more than a mention.

Outside the Tours region two groups stand out among a mass of provincial work which varied from district to district according to the different influences and environment. In the South East the painters of the court of Savoy were attracted by Italy and in particular, as in the time of Christine de Pisan, by

Lombardy, with which the court was linked by political and family ties. The art of Savoy was, however, fundamentally French, like the airs attached to the Italian (and French) songs in the *Chansonnier* of Jean de Montchenu, the apostolic protonotary, who belonged to the household of Jean-Louis of Savoy, Bishop of Geneva, and who later became Bishop of Viviers (Pl. LXXXIII): the *Chansonnier* may have been decorated by the painter of the Hours of Louis of Savoy, Jean-Louis's brother (Fig. 85). In the North, near Lille, in the territories of Jean de Wavrin, who was counsellor to Philip the Good, one artist in particular deserves to be singled out. A Flemish artist, he does not strictly speaking belong in this study, but as he illustrated a copy of the *Champion des Dames* by Martin Lefranc, provost of Lausanne and secretary to the Antipope Felix V (Amadeus VIII of Savoy), and as three out of his six surviving manuscripts are in the South East, it is probable that he worked for a while in the region of the Alps. It is enough here simply to mention this witty, elegant and lively artist whose tinted drawings possess a clearness of line which points the way forward to the high achievements soon to be recorded by the art of engraving (p. 93).

René of Anjou

René is a lonely figure. Although he retained something of the uneasiness of the Maître de Rohan (he knew him in his youth at the court of his mother Yolanda), which led him to meditate on death and the after-life and the mystery of the human estate, of which our world is the symbol, yet he expressed it in an entirely different way, by means that were pictorial in the strict sense. The experiments of the Flemish painters interested him and he had at his court several artists from the Low Countries, among them possibly the Maître de Jouvenel— supposing that he was a Fleming, which is open to doubt—who collaborated with him on a *Théséide* now in Vienna. Hence René's intense curiosity about the problems of chiaroscuro, which in his work is not so much a mere technical preoccupation as the expression of an attitude of mind, of the deepest chords of his soul. The nature of his sensibility is revealed by the text of his *Livre du Cœur d'amour épris*, which to us may appear insipid, but which is redeemed by the beauty of the illustrations. Before René no

86 – LOVE HANDS RENÉ OF ANJOU'S HEART TO DESIRE. RENÉ OF ANJOU, LIVRE DU CŒUR D'AMOUR ÉPRIS (VIENNA, OESTERREICHISCHE NATIONALBIBLIOTHEK, MS. 2597, F. 2)

French painter had mastered the infinite variety of light, nor dared to express, not so much by colour as by the language of light and shade, the inmost secrets and emotions of the heart. Two pages that are famous for this quality establish him as a great artist, among the most sensitive and inspired painters of all time (Figs. 86-87).

In the *Livre des tournois* René appears in a very different light (Pl. LXXXIV): as a brilliant lover of spectacles, who handles his compositions with the authority of a professional decorator, the assured line of a heraldic painter and a rare feeling for mass and volume. The latter quality he owed partly to direct observation, but

87 – CŒUR READS THE INSCRIPTION ON THE ENCHANTED
FOUNTAIN. RENÉ OF ANJOU, LIVRE DU CŒUR D'AMOUR ÉPRIS
(VIENNA, OESTERREICHISCHE NATIONALBIBLIOTHEK, MS. 2597,
F. 15)

also—as certain details of costume and landscape, especially in the *Cœur d'amour épris*, prove—to his familiarity with the French romances of chivalry illustrated in Italy in the late 14th and early 15th centuries.

North and South thus meet in the work of this great connoisseur, and it seems all the harder to dissociate the painter from the patron because detailed study shows that unlike any of his contemporaries, beginning with Fouquet, he can never be confused with anyone else. René gathered round him a circle of advisers and painters, such as the author of a remarkable *Livre de la chasse* (p. 84), but he had

neither pupils nor a workshop. That is why, so far as we know, he had no followers and no imitators.

Jean Colombe

Jean Colombe was born at Bourges about the middle of the 15th century and lived there until he entered the service of Duke Charles of Savoy. In about 1485 he completed for the Duke the *Très riches heures* which the Limbourg brothers had long ago begun for Jean de Berry. His family included the great sculptor Michel, who may have been his brother, and François, another painter, who was doubtless his son. All three were famous artists and they took part in such great enterprises as the church at Brou and the cathedral at Nantes. Jean himself was, it appears, very active. Overwhelmed by commissions, he employed assistants and pupils to finish jobs for which he himself had made only the rough sketch and his work, which is a mixture of the very good and the very bad, gives a general impression of haste and negligence. At his best he ranks among the finest French painters of the late 15th century.

From Fouquet, who was possibly his master and in any case his model, he learned the importance of the setting, and although he does not achieve the luminous and spacious unity or the balance which distinguish the Tours master, he delights like him in tricks of perspective and carries to extremes the latter's researches into colour. He studied the effect of light coming from behind the object, of penumbras, the dancing reflections of flames, stormy skies, and snow (Fig. 88); and he used with profusion the gold which Fouquet had handled so discreetly. Everything in his work is exaggerated, and his painting reflects a personality whose impetuosity is revealed by the notes which he scattered, in the guise of inscriptions, over the hems of garments and the cornices of buildings. Beside the motto of his workshop—"Omnis spiritus laudet Dominum", taken from Psalm 150—we find furious exclamations like "Time wasted for Colombe", or "I'm wasting my time working for you". He was indeed wasting the time which artists of his class sometimes have to devote to rough preliminary work that will be completed for them by others.

His figures are hard, with closed faces, heavy eyes and low foreheads; they are dressed in long, thick robes or weighed down with armour; they gesticulate, are pompous and grandiloquent, or else crowd to-

gether in compact, monolithic groups. His architectural settings are generally very bare, bordering on streets whose haunted emptiness recalls a landscape by Chirico, or disappearing under tier upon tier of arcades, figured bas-reliefs and fantastic inlays inspired by the most elaborate Roman survivals. Berrichon that he was, Colombe lost sight of the calm and smiling elegance, with its restraint and unfailing concern for sound composition and perfect execution, which had been the hallmark of French Gothic painting from the Psalter of St. Louis to Fouquet; which the Mosan, Pol de Limbourg, had mastered; and which even the Maître de Rohan had remembered whenever he consented to abandon the decorative hotch-potch of colours by which he imitated the discoveries in perspective and volume that so engrossed his contemporaries. Colombe thus passed from one extreme to the other: the effect of his uncontrollable temperament, but also of the beginnings of a passion which in the 16th century was to trouble French literature and religion, beneath the calm and brilliant surface of the art of the court. Colombe is a precursor of the school of Fontainebleau, in so far as it escaped the total domination of Italy, and after it of Antoine Caron. He is at the root of the mannerism which was to persist in France until well on in the 17th century. It is to this, rather than to his hurried and unequal œuvre, that he owes his importance. He none the less achieved several successes. The magnificent sketches in a copy of the *Guerre de Troie* decorated for Aymar de Poitiers in about 1500 (Pl. LXXXV) show what he could have done had he been a patient man, kept his head under pressure of work, taken more pride in his talent, and had fewer worries about money. Another of his works is the Laval Hours, certain pages of which have been attributed to Fouquet—the robust figures of the Sibyls and the very living portrait of Louis de Laval (Pl. LXXXVI), to mention only the best miniatures in this sumptuous volume. Pictures like these place Colombe among the masters of French illumination, far behind Fouquet, it is true, but far ahead of the illuminator who concludes the series and to whom we must now turn.

Jean Bourdichon

Jean Bourdichon has been greatly overpraised; and in his own day he enjoyed an unprecedented notoriety.

88 – HANNIBAL CROSSES THE ALPS. ROBERTO DELLA PORTA. ROMULÉON, CIRCA 1490 (BIBLIOTHÈQUE NATIONALE, MS. FR, 365, F. 19 V.)

Painstaking, calm and pleasing as he was, he seems to have worked largely on his own, or at least to have exercised a strict supervision over the work of his assistants, and unlike Colombe he is the perfect representative of official art, with its discipline, its flattery and its comfortable refusal to disturb. Nothing could be duller or more insipid than the famous *Grandes Heures* which he painted for Anne of Britany, in spite of its praiseworthy technical mastery (Pl. LXXXVII). But he is open to criticism even there: his borders strewn with naturalistic flowers, plants and insects are copied from illuminations of the Ghent-Bruges school but come nowhere near the prodigious virtuosity of their models. From Fouquet he learned to use gold to impart a sparkle to his draperies, but like Colombe he misused it and in his

89 – THE VIRGIN MARY. HOURS OF CHARLES VIII, CIRCA 1485 (BIBLIOTHÈQUE NATIONALE, MS. LAT. 1370, F. 36)

90 – THE TRIUMPH OF LOVE. PETRARCH, TRIOMPHES, CIRCA 1500 (BIBLIOTHÈQUE NATIONALE, MS. FR. 594, F. 348 V.)

hands the spuriousness of the formula is obvious. His night effects, which for some reason or other have been so greatly admired, are not as good as Colombe's or, in an earlier period, the beautiful Golgotha in the *Très riches heures*; they are unintelligently done, mere tracts of unrelieved blackness. And yet Bourdichon was not without solid merits, even though he lacked originality of temperament. So far as it can be dated, his youthful work has freshness and taste, not to mention the conscientiousness that he was never to lose, and we must take care not to accuse him of having been spoiled by success. The Hours of Charles VIII, in tinted grisaille, which was painted in about 1485 (Fig. 89), and the Hours of Francis of Vendôme, which may be a little earlier and seems to be his first known work, display a sobriety which he inherited from Fouquet and a feeling for colour which he owed to Colombe, already accompanied by the innate coldness which was to lead him into academism.

The "Rouen" School

The "Rouen" school is so called because its centre was Cardinal Georges d'Amboise, Archbishop of Rouen and a minister of Louis XII, who commissioned the splendid mass of buildings, now destroyed, which formed the Château de Gaillon; but its association with Rouen is purely accidental and contributed nothing to the character of its painting, which was the offspring both of Colombe and of Bourdichon. The "Rouen" artists wildly exaggerated Colombe's defects and accepted them as formulas. On the eve of the Italian invasion which marks the beginning of the 16th century and the end of our study, we should spare a thought for their pompous rhetoric, which was so much in keeping with the times of Jean Lemaire de Belges. Empty though it is, it is of interest as the expression of an aspect of contemporary taste, that of the rhetoricians. The "Rouen" school liked easy, tawdry effects; a profusion of gold and bright

colours; large, full-page compositions packed with superbly-dressed figures. They cared for nothing but opulence and brilliance (Fig. 90). Their chief weakness lay in the fact that they included in their number no painter of real talent; they were mere decorators, but they kept alive, however unintelligently, a tradition of French design which was filtered and purified by the Italians who came to work on Francis I's palace, and which combined with the Italian contribution to form the so-called school of Fontainebleau that was to prove so fruitful and so full of promise for the future. The mere existence of the "Rouen" artists, and the kind of passive resistance that they opposed to their Italian colleagues, are important in themselves; that is why they are mentioned here, although it was their fault that French illumination ended in emptiness and noise. Even so, we have not quite finished. At the beginning of the 16th century, in spite of the invention of printing, the very finest books were still written and decorated by hand, and the best printed books were on parchment and contained hand-coloured engravings. Nor did easel-painting immediately supplant illumination. The illuminators of the period are, however, isolated figures of widely different character. There were the mysterious Maître de Moulins, who may or may not be identical with Jean Perréal (p. 89), and the so-called Painter of Charles VIII, whose portraits, which are really anonymous, are concealed between the leaves of an imitation Book of Hours: which shows that the tradition which connected painting, and even portrait-painting (Pl. LXXXVIII), with the book was still extremely powerful in France. Another was the painter of Charles of Angoulême (Pl. LXXXIX), a discerning colourist whose work is so strangely dry that one senses in it the influence of the copper-engravings which he was not ashamed to insert into the Book of Hours executed for Francis I's father. Last of all comes a court painter (Pl. XC) whose cold and laboured pictures, harmonious but lifeless as they are, no longer have anything in common with the art of illumination and bring us down to the years round 1530, when French printing was already in its heyday.

GASTON PHÉBUS OFFERS HIS WORK TO THE HUNTSMEN. Gaston Phébus, *Le Livre de la chasse*, circa 1450 (Bibliothèque Nationale, Ms. fr. 1291, f. 5)

BIBLIOGRAPHICAL COMMENTARY

No general account of French illumination exists, apart from the chapters devoted to it in André Michel's *Histoire de l'art*, where A. Haseloff dealt with Romanesque and the beginning of Gothic (vol. I, pt. 2, p. 77, and vol. II, pt. I, 1906, p. 298), and P. Durrieu with later Gothic (vol. III, pt. I, 1907, p. 101, and vol. IV, pt. 2, 1911, p. 701).

Two recent works on illumination in general are: L. Réau, *Histoire de la peinture au Moyen âge, la miniature*, Melun, 1946; D. Diringer, *The Illuminated Book*, London, 1958.

Western illumination is the subject of A. Boeckler's *Abendländische Miniaturen bis zum Ausgang der romanischen Zeit*, Berlin, 1930, and of the chapters by C. Nordenfalk in A. Grabar and C. Nordenfalk, *Early Medieval Painting*, Skira, 1957, and *Romanesque Painting*, Skira, 1958. See also A. Boeckler and A. Schmid in Milkau, *Handbuch*, 1952, I, pp. 249 ff.

J. Dupont has given a general account of Gothic illumination and painting in *Gothic Painting*, Skira, 1954 (with C. Gnudi); for French painting in the 14th and 15th centuries, see Ch. Jacques (Sterling), *Les Peintres du Moyen âge*, Paris, 1941, and P. A. Lemoisne, *La Peinture française à l'époque gothique*, Paris, 1931; for the 15th century, see G. Ring, *A Century of French Painting*, London, 1949. Specialised studies of French Gothic illumination are: G. Graf Vitzthum, *Die Pariser Miniaturmalerei von der Zeit des hl. Ludwig bis zu Philipp von Valois und ihr Verhältnis zur Malerei in Nordwesteuropa*, Leipzig, 1907; H. Martin, *La Miniature française du XIIIe au XVe siècle*, Paris, 1923; *Les Miniaturistes français*, Paris, 1906; A. Blum and Ph. Lauer, *La Miniature aux XVe et XVIe siècles*, Paris, 1930. Millard Meiss's important study of painting in the time of Jean de Berry is nearing completion.

The following deal with the illuminated MSS. in particular collections: Ph. Lauer, *Les Enluminures romanes des manuscrits de la Bibliothèque nationale*, Paris, 1927; H. Martin, *Les Joyaux de l'Enluminure à la Bibliothèque nationale*, Paris, 1928; A. Boinet, *Les Manuscrits à peintures de la Bibliothèque Sainte-Geneviève*, Paris, 1921; H. Martin and Ph. Lauer, *Les Principaux manuscrits à peintures de la Bibliothèque de l'Arsenal*, Paris, 1929; C. Oursel, *Les Manuscrits à peintures de la Bibliothèque de Dijon*, Paris, 1923; L. Morel-Payen, *Les plus beaux manuscrits à peintures ... de la Bibliothèque de Troyes*, Troyes, 1935. Similar works have been published on the great libraries outside France, and they include many French MSS.: see *Liste des recueils de Fac-similés de la Bibliothèque nationale*, 1935 (new edition in preparation). Further information will be found in the catalogues of exhibitions, including: for French illumination in general, *Bibliothèque nationale, Les manuscrits à peintures en France du VIIe au XIIe siècle*, 1954; ... *du XIIIe au XVIe siècle*, 1955;—for French illumination in particular regions, Limoges, 1950; Arras, 1951; Troyes, 1951; Bourges, 1951; Toulouse, 1954;—for illumination in general, *Abendländische Buchmalerei*, Vienna, 1952; *Gyllene Böcker*, Stockholm-Copenhagen, 1952; *Mostra storica nazionale della miniatura*, Rome, 1953. To these we may

now add P. Vaillant's 12 colour plates, with introduction, of *Enluminures cartusiennes*, Roissard of Grenoble, 1959, and C. Oursel's *Miniature à Cîteaux*, Protat of Mâcon, 1959.

The following catalogues by V. Leroquais deal with the liturgical MSS., most of which are illuminated, in French libraries: *Livres d'heures*, 1927; *Sacramentaires et missels*, 1924; *Bréviaires*, 1934; *Pontificaux*, 1937; *Psautiers*, 1940–41.

The illustrations to my own book are almost entirely derived from MSS. in public collections in France, and in particular from MSS. in the Bibliothèque Nationale. The reason for this is not only one of convenience: the Parisian and provincial libraries of France contain the essential material for the subject and include quite enough examples for the purpose of a general survey such as this. My survey makes not the slightest claim to be exhaustive: the MSS. I have referred to simply mark the major stages in a development which, for many reasons, could not possibly be followed in detail. I have supplemented it by the explanatory and bibliographical notes which follow: though reduced to bare essentials, they will enable the reader to find other books and articles on the subjects in question.

These notes refer to the pages of my essay. They include the pressmarks of the manuscripts mentioned but not reproduced in the text, which are also listed in the index. The index also includes all the manuscripts reproduced in the book, in colour and in black and white. Pressmarks which are not preceded by the name of a town or of a library belong to MSS. in the Bibliothèque Nationale.

The illustrations are drawn not only from French manuscripts but from a variety of other works of art, both paintings and sculptures, to which—rightly or wrongly—I have thought it useful to compare them. French medieval art cannot be isolated from the art of neighbouring countries and the number of these comparisons could usefully have been increased.

The study of iconography has no place in these pages, which are concerned only with questions of form. Iconography is in itself of considerable interest and may on occasion prove helpful in the study of forms, but it is not invariably so and may sometimes actually obscure the solution of formal problems. It is in any case a separate subject, which could not be discussed here in detail. And yet I feel bound to say a few words about the distinction between Romanesque iconography and Gothic. Romanesque images are based on the conception of the world as a "forest of symbols"; man is surrounded by appearances and human life is entirely subordinated to the after-life, to the heavenly realities towards which it aspires. It follows that these appearances are in themselves of no importance and are of interest only as references to the universal. The consequences of this view have been recorded above (p. 11). The Gothic 13th century, on the other hand, witnessed the development—along with experimental sciences such as medicine, and not without opposition—of a theology which took account of man and his nature, of his acts and their motives, and of his surroundings in this world, which were seen as the reflection, and no longer as the veil or symbol, of eternal realities. In the Romanesque period men were brought up on Plato, in the Gothic period they discovered Aristotle. Hence the importance given to moral values, for which the Dominican St. Thomas Aquinas reserved an important place in his *Summa*, and to nature. The contents of books were profoundly modified in consequence. A work like the *Bible moralisée* is Gothic not only in form but in spirit, and it is as typically Dominican as St. Thomas's *Summa*. The subject could be pursued further, and it would be possible to demonstrate the formation of an iconography, religious and secular alike, intended for the layman. It will suffice, in this context to state that the evolution of plastic forms which occurred in the Gothic period was matched by a comparable evolution of iconography; but there is no doubt that the changes in form and iconography are simply the two complementary aspects of a single historical process.

PAGE 11

On the origins of medieval perspective, see A. Grabar, in *Cahiers archéologiques*, 1945, p. 15.

PAGE 12

Terence from Angers: Leyden, Voss. 38. Missal from Saint-Maur: Lat. 12054. *Lives and miracles* of St. Maurus: Lat. 3778 and Troyes, MS. 2273. *Lives* of SS. Valerius and Philibertus: Boulogne, MS. 106. *Life* of St. Quintinus: Saint-Quentin, Basilica.

See also F. Wormald, "Some Illustrated Lives of the Saints", *Bulletin of the John Rylands Library*, 1952, pp. 248 ff.

PAGE 13

Gospel-book of Gaudiosus: Angers, MS. 24. Gospel-lectionary of Nivardus: Lat. 1126 (see C. Nordenfalk, "A Travelling Milanese Artist in France", in *Arte del primo millennio*, 1953, pp. 374 ff.). Lectionary from Montmajour: Lat. 889.

PAGES 14–15

Lectionary from Saint-Martial: see J. Porcher, in *Spätantike und Byzanz*, 1951, p. 189. Missal from Saint-Denis: Fräulein S. Schulten has demonstrated its connection with Saint-Vaast in an unpublished thesis, *Die Buchmalerei im Kloster Saint-Vaast d'Arras im XI. Jahrh.*, 1954, and in *Münchner Jahrb.*, vii, 1956, p. 49.

PAGES 15–16

Lectionary from Saint-Germain-des-Prés: Lat. 11751 (for the whole group of MSS. from this abbey, see Y. Deslandres, in *Scriptorium*, 1955, pp. 3, 55).

PAGES 17–18

St. Gregory's *Moralia*: Cambrai, MS. 215. Gospel-books of Odbert: New York, Pierpont Morgan Library, MS. 333; Saint-Omer, MSS. 342 *bis* and 56 (the latter, which contains the Christ copied from Boulogne MS. 11, comes from the Cathedral chapter and is probably not by Odbert's own hand, although under his direct influence). Aratus's *Phaenomena*: Boulogne, MS. 188; Leyden, Voss. lat. 8⁰ 79. *Lives* of SS. Bertinus, Folquinus and others: Boulogne, MS. 107.

PAGES 19–20

Miracles of St. Vedastus: Arras, MS. 686. It is seldom possible, in this early period, to watch an atelier at work, and this is why I felt bound to linger over it. If, as is probable, the painters were also the scribes, it follows that they were monks and belonged to the abbey. But we can hardly speak of them as a "school" since their period of activity obviously lasted only a few years.
For the Bayeux Tapestry and its origin, see F. Wormald, in *The Bayeux Tapestry*, London, 1957.
Gospel-book from Mortain: Saint-Lô, Archives, MS. 1. *Works* of SS. Augustine, Ambrose and Jerome: Avranches, MSS. 72, 75, 76, 90; Lat. 2079 and 2639. Characteristic MSS. from Lower Normandy were brought together in the exhibition of *Manuscrits*

à peintures du VIIe au XIIe siècle, Nos. 196–203. O. Pächt has given a convincing demonstration of their influence on English illumination in his study of two MSS. signed by a painter named Hugo ("Hugo Pictor", *The Bodleian Library Record*, iii, 1950, p. 96). The relationship between MSS. from Lower Normandy and from England has recently received very full treatment in C. R. Dodwell's *The Canterbury School of Illumination*, 1954, pp. 6 ff.

PAGES 20–21

For William of Saint-Calais and Durham, see H. Swarzenski, in *Form und Inhalt*: *Festschrift O. Schmitt*, p. 89. St. Jerome's *Letters*, from Cîteaux: Dijon, MS. 289. St. Gregory's *Moralia*: Dijon, MSS. 168–170. For illumination at Cîteaux, see C. Oursel, *La miniature du XIIe siècle à l'abbaye de Cîteaux*, Dijon, 1926 (new edition in preparation).

PAGE 22

English Psalter, of unknown origin, imitated by the Vendôme MS.: British Museum, Cotton MS. Tiberius C. vi, f. 14. Gospel-book from Senones: Lat. 9392.

PAGES 22–24

Gospel-lectionary from Lorraine: Lat. 9453. Gospel-books from Saint-Vanne: Verdun, MSS. 52 (second half of the 11th century), 43 (first half of the 12th century). Lectionaries: Verdun, MSS. 1, 119 (*circa* 1100). Lectionary from Cluny: Nouv. acq. lat. 2246 (C. Nordenfalk has discovered a remarkable MS. from Cluny at Parma; *Romanesque Painting*, pp. 188–90).

PAGE 26

Of the decoration of the Albi Psalter Mme M. M. Gauthier observes that it is not of the kind ordinarily found in Romanesque MSS. from the Midi ("Les décors vermiculés", in *Cahiers de Civilisation médiévale*, i, 1958, p. 358). Although we know of no further instance of this decoration, there does exist other evidence of the same kind which confirms my interpretation (see pp. 28–9).

PAGE 27

The Bible from Saint-Martial, Limoges (Fig. 25), is of uncertain date. I attribute it to the 10th century, as its decoration seems to require; but Professor B. Bischoff attributes it to the 9th century, on the grounds of the handwriting. We must remember that

the writing of Bibles is sometimes archaizing (see p. 30, on the Bible from Saint-Aubin).

PAGE 29

Many examples of the angel with the bent head occur in Byzantine painting, from the 7th century specimen in Santa Maria Antiqua, Rome, to the St. Michael of our Fig. 24, which dates from *circa* 1078 and so is contemporary with the Josephus from Toulouse, to which it was first compared in the exhibition, *Byzance et la France médiévale*, held at the Bibliothèque Nationale in 1958. The comparison was not very well received, but it seems to me to be corroborated by the several parallel cases cited here, which show that forms from the Eastern Mediterranean were entering Languedoc from the end of the 11th century onwards. It is interesting to see how all these forms, and particularly the angel, were transmuted on entering the Romanesque world.

PAGE 30

The frescoes at Vic have often been reproduced, most recently by Mme L. Brion-Guerry, *Fresques romanes de France*, 1958, figs. 49–54.
The Ascension window at Le Mans is reproduced in *Le Vitrail français*, 1958, pl. IX, p. 82.
For the paintings at Saint-Aubin, Angers, see *Anjou roman*, 1959, pp. 179–219.

PAGE 32

Sacramentary from Liège: Lat. 819.

PAGES 33–34

The relationship between the sculpture of Northern Italy and that of France has recently been examined by R. Salvini, in *Kunstgeschichtliche Studien für H. Kaufmann*, 1956, pp. 67 ff., and in *Wiligelmo e le origini della scultura romanica*, Milan, 1956. On the date of the pulpit in Sant'Ambrogio, see R. Jullian, in *Revue archéologique*, 1958, p. 189.
Bible from Saint-Bénigne: Dijon, MS. 2.
Abbot Jarento's contacts with Spain are specially mentioned in the Necrology of Saint-Bénigne (Dijon, MS. 634, under 20 Sept.).

PAGES 34–35

The "Mosan" manner reached as far as the Rhineland, and may even have originated there. On the other hand, the influence of the excellent draughtsmen of

Saint-Bertin seems to have extended in another direction, down to the 13th century. A well-known drawing in Rheims, MS. 672, f.1*v* (reproduced, for example, in P. Neveux and E. Dacier, *Les Richesses des bibliothèques provinciales de France*, ii, 1932, pl. XXVI), is not necessarily from Rheims or even from Saint-Bertin (although the latter seems probable); but the interesting illustrations in a *Speculum virginum* from Clairvaux (Troyes, MS. 252) are certainly descended from Saint-Bertin (reproduced by C. Nordenfalk, *Romanesque Painting*, p. 162). Bible from Saint-Bertin: Lat. 16743–16746.

PAGE 36

Life of St. Rictrude (first half of the 11th century): Douai, MS. 849.

PAGES 36–37

Savalo and the Saint-Amand MSS. in general have been closely examined by A. Boutemy in a series of articles in *Revue belge d'archéologie et d'histoire de l'art*, (1939, pp. 299 ff.; 1942, pp. 131 ff., 299 ff.). St. Hilary's *Works*: Lat. 1699. Peter Lombard's *Sentences*: Valenciennes, MS. 186.
For the Anchin MSS., see A. Boutemy, in *Scriptorium*, ix, 1957, p. 234.

PAGE 38

If we conclude that Middle Eastern forms were transmitted by ivories rather than by MSS., it is because it is hard to see how the latter could have been known in the West: those we have, like the MSS. of the Macedonian Renaissance referred to here, reached France at a much later period. Typical of the ivories that may have served this purpose is the Joel in the Claudius Côte Collection at Lyon (Volbach, *Elfenbeinarbeiten*, 1952, fig. 245; 11th century). W. Koehler has demonstrated the importance of Byzantine art in the Romanesque West, especially at Saint-Amand: "Byzantine Art in the West", *Dumbarton Oaks Papers*, i, 1940, pp. 62–87.

PAGE 40

Bible from Saint-Sulpice: Bourges, MS. 3. Greek Psalter in Paris: Gr. 139.

PAGE 41

Bible of Manerius: Sainte-Geneviève, MSS. 8–10. Bible from Sens: Sens, MS. 1. Bible from Saint-

CHARLES VIII AND THE KNIGHTS OF ST. MICHAEL. *Statutes of the Order of St. Michael*, 1493 (Bibliothèque Nationale, Ms. fr. 14363, f. 3)

Germain-des-Prés: Lat. 11535. The most recent discussion of these Bibles is by C. R. Dodwell, *The Canterbury School of Illumination*, pp. 81 ff., where they are definitively attributed to France. A Gratian in the Dyson Perrins Collection (1st sale-catalogue, December 1958, lot 4) is closely related to the Bible from Saint-André-au-Bois, which has been studied by A. Boutemy in *Scriptorium*, 1951, p. 222. This group of MSS., which is of capital importance for the origin of Gothic art, is still inadequately known.

The origin of the acanthus is in fact something of a mystery. It may be compared to the decoration of certain ivories, among them a 12th-century Byzantine (or Islamic) box in the Victoria and Albert Museum (5471/1859, reproduced by M. H. Longhurst, *Cata-logue of Carvings*, i, 1927, fig. 26); but it must be admitted that the comparison is not very convincing. Examples from Sicily are of no assistance here. The acanthus often occurs beside the multiple concentric scrolls, inhabited by little white lions, which probably come from Monte Cassino; and its Mediterranean origin is confirmed by the iconography (see pp. 39–40).

On the (temporary) influence exercised by St. Bernard, see a note in the catalogue of an exhibition, Saint Bernard et l'art des Cisterciens, held at Dijon in 1953, pp. 19–21; for the same tendency in architecture see Hanno Hahn, *Die frühe Baukunst der Zistercienser*, 1957, and M. Aubert, in *Cahiers de civilisation médiévale*, i, 1958, p. 153.

PAGES 44–45

The connection between the "Life of Christ" and the windows at Chartres was pointed out by C. R. Morey, in *The Pierpont Morgan Library, Exhibition of Illuminated Manuscripts*, 1933, p. xiv.
Suger's treatise has recently been published, with an English translation and a long introduction, by E. Panofsky, *Abbot Suger, On the Abbey Church of Saint-Denis*, Princeton, 1946.
Bible moralisée: second part of a copy now divided between the Bodleian Library (Auct. B. IV, 6) and the British Museum (Harley 1526–1527). Other copies are in the Chapter Library at Toledo (with part in the Pierpont Morgan Library) and in the National-bibliothek at Vienna (A. de Laborde, *La Bible moralisée conservée à Oxford, Paris et Londres*, 1911–1927). Psalter of St. Louis: Lat. 10525 (Leroquais, *Psautiers*, vol. ii, p. 101).

PAGE 46

Gospel-lectionary from the Sainte-Chapelle: Lat. 8892 and 17326.
Guillaume le Clerc, *Bestiaire*: Fr. 14970.

PAGES 47–48

Psalter of St. Louis: Leyden, University Library. Ingeburga's Psalter: H. Swarzenski, following G. Haseloff (*Psalterillustration im XIII. Jahrh.*, 1938, p. 14), compared it with the Anchin Missal (*Monuments of Romanesque Art*, 1954, figs. 541–542). On the connection between the windows at Laon and others in the same region, see L. Grodecki, in *Le Vitrail français*, 1958, p. 118, referring to researches by Deuchler. Whatever the importance of this connection, which seems to be obvious, it is only right to observe that the "Anchin" pictorial style occurs nowhere else in the North of France and seems to be isolated and imported, at least where illumination is concerned. The treatment of folds in drapery is comparable to that of the Rhenish illuminators (Cologne, Speyer), and the expressions of the faces and the colours are strikingly similar to those, for example, of the famous Virgin in the *Liber matutinalis* from Scheyern (Boeckler, *Deutsche Malerei vorgotischer Zeit*, 1953, fig. 62). For the latest discussion, see O. Homburger, in *Formositas Romanica*, Frauenfeld, 1958, p. 35.
Psalter of Christina: Copenhagen, Royal Library, Gl. kgl. Samml. 1606, 4⁰.

PAGES 48–49

Roman de Troie: Fr. 1610. *Histoire de Jérusalem*: Fr. 9081. *Conte de Méliacin*: Fr. 1633. Breviary from Froidmont: Paris, École des Beaux-Arts, donation Masson, No. 349 (see *Bibliothèque de l'École des chartes*, 1943, p. 258).

PAGES 49–50

Gratian's *Decretum*: Tours, MS. 558. The latest account of everything to do with Honoré is in E. G. Millar's facsimile edition of one of his finest MSS. (*An Illuminated Manuscript of La Somme le Roy*, Oxford, 1953). Paris *Chansonnier*: reproduced by Y. Rokseth, *Polyphonies du XIIIe siècle*, 1935–1939.

PAGE 51

Bible historiale: Many copies, including Lat. 8; Arsenal, MS. 5059 (copied by the Parisian scribe Jean de Papeleu in 1317); Troyes, MS. 59; Sainte-Geneviève, MSS. 20–21. *Vie de saint Denis*: Fr. 2090–2092 (reproduced by H. Martin in 1908). Another copy of the Latin text, drawn but not painted and doubtless later, more complete: Lat. 5286. The well-known *Roman de Fauvel* (Fr. 146) belongs to the same family.
The centre at Avignon, like the centre in Languedoc, is mentioned here only in passing. If there ever was an Avignon school, it can scarcely be distinguished from the Paris school and seems to have derived nothing whatsoever from Italy; French and Italian painters worked side by side in the papal city without developing a common style. It was the same in Languedoc; beside MSS. of the Italian type, but without any contact with them, the work of a painter (or workshop) of purely Northern formation can be distinguished at Toulouse, *circa* 1350–1370. Its style is a specifically local variant but derives directly from the paintings referred to on the preceding page. The group includes a Missal made for the Friars Hermits of Saint-Augustin (Toulouse, MS. 91; dated 1362), and portraits of *capitouls* in the *Annales capitulaires* for 1369–1370 (Toulouse, Musée des Augustins); see also a Bartholomaeus Anglicus in the Bibliothèque Sainte-Geneviève (MS. 1029) and a *Breviari d'Amor* finished at Toulouse in 1354, now MS. 2563 in the Nationalbibliothek at Vienna (Fr. Unterkircher, *Inventar der illumin. Handschriften*, 1957, p. 74). For the Avignon miniaturists, see H. Labande, in *Gazette des Beaux-Arts*, i, 1907, pp. 213, 289. For relations with

Bohemia, see A. Kutal, "L'Art du Moyen âge en Bohème et en Moravie", in *L'Art ancien en Tchécoslovaquie*, exhibition, Paris, 1957, with bibliography, especially under No. 112. For Languedoc, see *Dix siècles d'enluminure et de sculpture en Languedoc*, exhibiton, Toulouse, 1954–1955, pp. 6–8 and pls. IX–X.

PAGE 52

Bible of Robert de Billyng: Lat. 11935.
The latest bibliographies of publications about Pucelle are given by E. Panofsky, *Early Netherlandish Painting*, 1953, pp. 32–35 and notes, and in *Les Manuscrits à peintures du XIIIe au XVIe siècle*, Nos. 106 ff.

PAGE 53

For the kalendar of the Belleville Breviary, see S. C. Cockerell, *The Book of Hours of Yolanda of Flanders*, London, 1905.
Mme Morand has just completed an important study of Pucelle, as yet unpublished, which will appear in England, and which will renew and at many points supplement our knowledge of the master.

PAGES 56–57

For the Maître aux Boqueteaux, see H. Martin, *La Miniature française du XIIIe au XVe siècle*, pp. 35 ff. For Charles V, see L. Delisle, *Recherches sur la librairie de Charles V*, 1907.
The question of Jean Bondol has been studied in detail by E. Panofsky, *Early Netherlandish Painting*, pp. 38–40.
Cité de Dieu: Fr. 22912–22913.

PAGES 57–58

Copy of the statutes of the "peintres et imagiers" of 1391 in Fr. 22119, f. 2, taken from the "Livre vert ancien" of the Chambre des Comptes, now lost.
The character of the "peintre de 1402" has been very accurately delineated by Bella Martens, *Meister Franke*, 1929, but the author of this excellent study was mistaken in believing that the painter, or rather the group of painters, was Parisian; in fact the stream runs in the opposite direction.
Boccaccio's *Femmes célèbres:* Fr. 598 and 12420.
Bible historiale; Fr. 159 and Arsenal, MSS. 5057–5058.

PAGES 58–59

Zebo da Firenze was identified by Otto Pächt. Note on Jean Lebègue with bibliography by J. Porcher in *Mélanges Franz Calot*, 1959; for Christine de Pisan's painter, see *Manuscrits à peintures en France du XIIIe au XVIe siècle*, p. 69 and Nos. 149–151.

PAGE 59

The bibliography of Jean de Berry and the pressmarks of all the MSS. referred to here are given in *Les Manuscrits à peintures*, as above, Nos. 180–196. The *Très belles heures de Notre-Dame* is now in the Bibliothèque Nationale, to which it was presented in 1957 by the late Baron Maurice de Rothschild: Nouv. acq. lat. 3093. For the *Grandes Heures*, Jacquemart de Hesdin and the Christ carrying the Cross in the Louvre, see O. Pächt, in *Revue des Arts*, vi, 1956, p. 149. Coëtivy Hours: Chester Beatty Library, Dublin.

PAGE 67

The works of the Maître de Boucicaut have been analysed in detail by E. Panofsky, *Early Netherlandish Painting*, pp. 54 ff. Bedford Hours: British Museum, Add. MS. 18850.
P. Durrieu once proposed to identify the Maître de Bedford with the Fleming Jacques Coene, who lived at Paris and worked on Milan Cathedral, but he did not afterwards insist on the suggestion, which cannot at present be verified *(Les Arts anciens de Flandre,* 1906, pp. 5 ff.).

PAGE 68

Térence des ducs: published by H. Martin, 1907. *Très riches heures:* reproduced by P. Durrieu, Paris, 1904.

PAGE 69

For the Maître de Rohan, see J. Porcher, *The Rohan Book of Hours*, London, 1959.

PAGES 70–71

Hours of Rouen use: Arsenal 1562. Jean de Courcy's Chronicle: Fr. 20124 and 6183 + 15459. Guillaume de Tyr: Fr. 2629.
K. Perls has reproduced all Fouquet's works, certain and uncertain, with a short introduction, in a work published in 1940. An excellent account of our knowledge of him has been given by Ch. Sterling, in *Art Bulletin*, xxviii, 1946, pp. 125 ff. The Manesse Verlag, of Zurich, is preparing a complete facsimile, in colours, of Fouquet's paintings, with introduction by J. Porcher.

PAGE 73

Boccaccio at Munich: reproduced by P. Durrieu, 1909.

PAGE 74

The Hours painted for Étienne Chevalier was dismembered during the 18th century in circumstances unknown. Forty-seven miniatures survive: they are divided between the Musée Condé, Chantilly (40), the Louvre (2), the Bibliothèque Nationale, the British Museum, Viscount Bearsted (London), M. G. Wildenstein and Mr. R. Lehmann (New York). See *Bulletin de la Société de l'histoire de l'art français*, 1947–1948.

PAGE 77

The Maître de Jouvenel des Ursins, whose character has not yet been completely defined, was one of the most important painters in 15th-century France, not so much for his own sake as for the position which he holds between France and the Flemish illuminators, and for the role which he played in the entourage of René of Anjou: that he was associated with René is beyond question, but the precise nature of the association has not so far been investigated. The King of Sicily was the centre of a numerous circle of artists, some of them Flemish, to whom we should unquestionably attribute such MSS. as the prayer-book of Jeanne de Laval, René's second wife (Poitiers, MS. 41); an *Arbre des batailles* by Honoré Bovet (Arsenal 2695); a *Grandes chroniques* (Châteauroux, MS. 5); and a *Livre des échecs* at Albi (MS. Rochegude 104). A *Roman du Graal* at Dijon (MS. 527) was exhibited among the MSS. of this group at the Bibliothèque Nationale in 1954 (No. 286) and as a Flemish MS. at Brussels in 1959 (No. 53): the double attribution is perfectly legitimate. The Maître de Jouvenel is also known as the Maître du Boccace de Genève, after one of his MSS.

PAGES 78–79

Mer des histoires: Lat. 4915. *Ordonnances* of Charles VII: Lat. 1577A. See *Revue française*, July, 1955.
The *Cité de Dieu* illuminated for Charles de Gaucourt has been attributed by Thuasne, on the basis of a letter of Gaguin, to "maître François" (see Laborde, *Cité de Dieu*, pp. 184, 397), and he has furthermore identified this François with one of Fouquet's sons who bore the same name. The identification is any-

thing but certain, if only in view of the gulf fixed between Jean and François; and yet Anne de Beaujeu's Book of Hours in the Charnacé Collection contains miniatures by both artists, which proves that François worked with Jean and gives us food for thought. Besides, he supplied books to the royal family *(Manuscrits à peintures du XIIIe au XVIe siècle*, Nos. 271–273).
Chansonnier of Jean de Montchenu: see J. Porcher, in *Trésors des bibliothèques de France*, 1946–1947. The shape of this volume (a double heart, whence it has sometimes been described as "cordiform") may perhaps be derived from the "two hearts miraculously conjoined" which "divers ambassadors" present to the altar of the chapel of Love in Martin Lefranc's *Champion des dames*, of which the best surviving copy, reproduced here, is at Grenoble (MS. 875).

PAGE 79

The space devoted to René of Anjou in this study in no way corresponds to the probable importance of this royal artist in French and even European art; but although we know something of his own work, thanks to the researches of P. Wescher (*Fouquet und seine Zeit*, 1945) and of O. Smital and E. Winkler (facsimile of the *Livre du Cœur d'amours épris*, 1927), the work of his entourage is entirely unexplored and for a proper understanding of them, as of René himself, we shall have to wait for the results of Otto Pächt's researches. René's painters appear to be familiars, perhaps advisers, not at all like the assistants of Fouquet or Colombe: which strengthens the view that René himself was a painter. See O. Pächt, "René d'Anjou et les Van Eyck", in *Cahiers de l'Association internationale des études françaises*, viii, 1956, p. 42.

PAGE 80

For Colombe, see P. Wescher's *Fouquet und seine Zeit* (quoted above). For his family in general and his famous brother, the sculptor, see P. Pradel, *Michel Colombe*, 1953.

PAGE 81

From the time of the French Revolution the *Guerre de Troie* illuminated for Aymar de Poitiers belonged to the Hermitage Library, to which it had been sold by Peter Dubrowski along with some 200 other MSS. from Saint-Germain-des-Prés. François Colombe, who was probably Jean's son, signed one of the small

MARTIN LEFRANC WRITING. Martin Lefranc, *Le Champion des Dames*, circa 1460 (Grenoble, Ms. 875, f. 21)

miniatures and may well have executed all of them in person. If so, his style was exactly like his father's. The Hours of Louis de Laval (1411–1489), governor of Champagne and Grand Master of the woods and forests of France, contains certain details which raise the difficult question of the relation between Fouquet and Colombe. The Bourges master was no match for the Tours master, but that is no excuse for depriving him of his best work, as has sometimes been done, in order to attribute it to the latter. Colombe's circle included the minor artists of the Central French school, among them the Jean de Montluçon who signed a Book of Hours now in the Arsenal (MS. 438).

PAGES 81–82

For Bourdichon, see P. Wescher *Fouquet und seine Zeit*, and the very complete study by R. Limousin (1954); the latter is undoubtedly too complete, but its reproductions are all the more useful for that reason. Bourdichon, as a celebrated artist, was clearly the head of a large workshop, which means that like Fouquet's his own personality is not easy to define. Useful and accurate information will be found in a thesis by Mlle Huillet d'Istria on Perréal (in the press): it is badly needed. The final period of French illumination is extremely confused and rigorous classification of MSS. will be needed (it has not yet progressed very far) before the subject can attract serious attention. Everything points to the fact that Bourdichon deliberately imitated the Flemish illuminators of the Ghent-Bruges school, which serves to distinguish him all the more clearly from Colombe.

For the "Rouen" school, see G. Ritter and J. Lafond, *Manuscrits à peintures de l'école de Rouen*, Rouen, 1913.

COLORPLATES

I – ST. THOMAS. *Lectionary of Saint-Martial, Limoges,* end of the 10th century (Bibliothèque Nationale, Ms. lat. 5301, f. 279 v.)

EA
ФѴ

THOMĀ
CUM
RE
LI
Q
VIS
DIS

cipulıſ adofficium apoſtolatuſelec

11 – CHRIST IN MAJESTY. *Missal of Saint-Denis*, middle of the 11th century (Bibliothèque Nationale, Ms. lat. 9436, f. 15 v.)

III – THE CRUCIFIXION. *Psalter-hymnary of Saint-Germain-des-Prés,* second half of the 11th century
(Bibliothèque Nationale, Ms. lat. 11550, f. 6)

IV – THE ASCENSION. *Lectionary of Saint-André, Le Cateau*, end of the 11th century (Cambrai, Ms. 528, f. 38 v.)

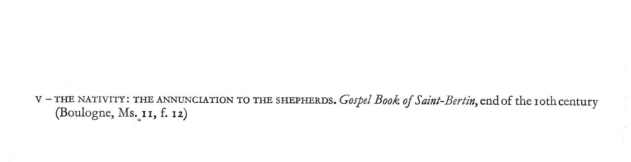

V – THE NATIVITY: THE ANNUNCIATION TO THE SHEPHERDS. *Gospel Book of Saint-Bertin*, end of the 10th century (Boulogne, Ms. 11, f. 12)

VI – ST. BERTINUS AND HIS COMPANIONS. *Vie des saints Bertin, Folquin, Silvin et Winnoc;* Saint-Bertin, circa 1000 (Boulogne, Ms. 107, f. 6 v.)

VII – ST. DIONYSIUS AND HIS COMPANIONS: MARTYRDOM OF ST. DIONYSIUS. *Gospels and Collects;* Saint-Bertin, circa 1000 (Saint-Omer, Ms. 342 *bis,* f. 63 v.)

VIII – ST. AUGUSTINE AND CHRIST: ALARDUS PRESENTS HIS BOOK TO ST. VEDASTUS. St. Augustine, *Confessions;* Saint-Vaast, Arras, first half of the 11th century (Arras, Ms. 548, f. 1 v.)

IX – THE SCRIBE PRESENTS HIS BOOK TO ST. MICHAEL. St. Clement, *Recognitiones;* Mont-Saint-Michel, beginning of the 11th century (Avranches, Ms. 50, f. 1)

X – ST. AUGUSTINE DISPUTES AGAINST FELICIANUS. *Oeuvres diverses des saints Jérôme, Augustin et Ambroise;* Mont-Saint-Michel, second half of the 11th century (Avranches, Ms. 72, f. 97)

XI – SOLOMON AND THE QUEEN OF SHEBA. St. Ambrose, *De Fide;* Saint-Évroult, end of the 11th century (Alençon, Ms. 11, f. 1 v.)

XII – DECORATED INITIAL. St. Gregory, *Moralia in Job;* Cîteaux, beginning of the 12th century (Dijon, Ms. 168, f. 4 v.)

Sanctissimi Ecclesiæ Doctoris Gregorii Papæ
ad Leandrum Episcopum Hispalensem Epistola
in expositionem libri Iob.

EVE
RENTIS
SIMO
ET SCĪSSIMO
FRĪ LEANDRO
CO EPO:
GREGORIƏ

SERVVS

SERVORV̄ DĪ;

XIII – ABBOT RICHER WRITES TO THE DICTATION OF SULPICIUS SEVERUS. *Recueil de textes sur saint Martin;* Saint-Martin, Metz, first half of the 12th century (Épinal, Ms. 73, f. 1)

PROEMIVM RICHERI ABBATIS
IN VITA SCI MARTINI

SVLPITIVS

XIV – THE ASCENSION. *Sacramentary of Saint-Étienne, Limoges,* circa 1100 (Bibliothèque Nationale, Ms. lat. 9438, f. 84 v.)

XV – DECORATED INITIAL. *Gradual of Saint-Michel, Gaillac,* 11th century (Bibliothèque Nationale, Ms. lat. 776, f. 5)

ELEVAVIANIMAMMEAM

XVI – DANCER. *Troper-Proser;* the Auch region, middle of the 11th century (Bibliothèque Nationale, Ms. lat. 1118, f. 114)

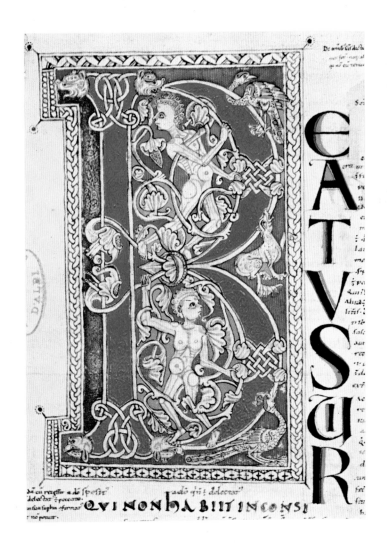

XVII – DECORATED INITIAL. *Glossed Psalter and Apocalypse;* Albi, second half of the 11th century (Albi, Ms. 45, f. 20)

XVIII – LOCUSTS. *Apocalypse of Saint-Sever*, middle of the 11th century (Bibliothèque Nationale, Ms. lat. 8878, f. 145)

QVOD VATES BELLVM CREVIT NON ESSE DVELLVM
EDIDIT & MVLTIS · VOBIS QVI CERNERE VVLTIS ·
EST IOSEPHVS DICTVS FERT LIBRVM CORPORE PICTVS ·

XX – ST. ALBINUS BLESSES THE BREAD AND WINE. *Vie de saint Aubin;* Angers, end of the 11th century
(Bibliothèque Nationale, Ms. nouv. acq. lat. 1390, f. 2)

XXI – A SCENE FROM THE LIFE OF ST. AUDOMARUS. *Vie de saint Omer*, end of the 11th century (Saint-Omer, Ms. 698, f. 34)

XXII – ST. MARK. *Gospel Book;* Corbie, end of the 11th century (Amiens, Ms. 24, f. 53)

XXIII – THE MASTER AND HIS SERVANT. *Lectionary of Rheims Cathedral,* end of the 11th century (Rheims, Ms. 294, f. 191)

DomC·VIIII·POST OCT PEN·

LC STI EV· SCDM MATHEV·

N IllO R·Dixit ihc dif
cipulif suif; Nemo poteft
duobuf dominif feruire;
Et cetera; OMEL VENER BEDE

PBRI· DE EAD L· IIX·

Nemo
poteft
duob;
domini
feruire:
quia ñ
ualet
fimul tranfi_
toria
na

& eter

XXIV – DANIEL IN THE LIONS' DEN. St. Jerome, *Explanatio in Prophetas;* Cîteaux, first half of the 12th century
(Dijon, Ms. 132, f. 2)

INCIPIT LIBER
EXPOSITIONIS·IN
DANIHELE·PPHAM;
TERCIO·REGNI
IOACHE·REGIS·IVDE

XXV – THE VIRGIN AND CHILD. St. Jerome, *Explanatio in Isaiam;* Cîteaux, first half of the 12th century (Dijon, Ms. 129, f. 4)

P OSTMORTEM

IOSUE CONSU

LUERUNT FILII

XXVII – THE SOUL OF LAMBERT, ABBOT OF SAINT-BERTIN, ASCENDS TO GOD. Saint-Bertin, circa 1125 (Boulogne, Ms. 46, f. 1)

XXVIII – BISHOP FRECULF: RABANUS MAURUS WITH HIS PUPILS. Rabanus Maurus, *Commentary on Exodus;* Anchin, second half of the 12th century (Douai, Ms. 339, f. 2 v.)

FINIVNT · CAPITVLA · LIBRI · PMI

INCIPIT · LIBER · RABA

NI · MAVRI · SVPER · EXO

DVM · AD · FREGVLFV · EPM.

EC · SVNT · NOMINA.

XXIX – ST. MATTHEW. *Gospel Book of Hénin-Liétard;* Saint-Bertin, middle of the 12th century
(Boulogne, Ms. 14, Vol. 1, f. 22 v.)

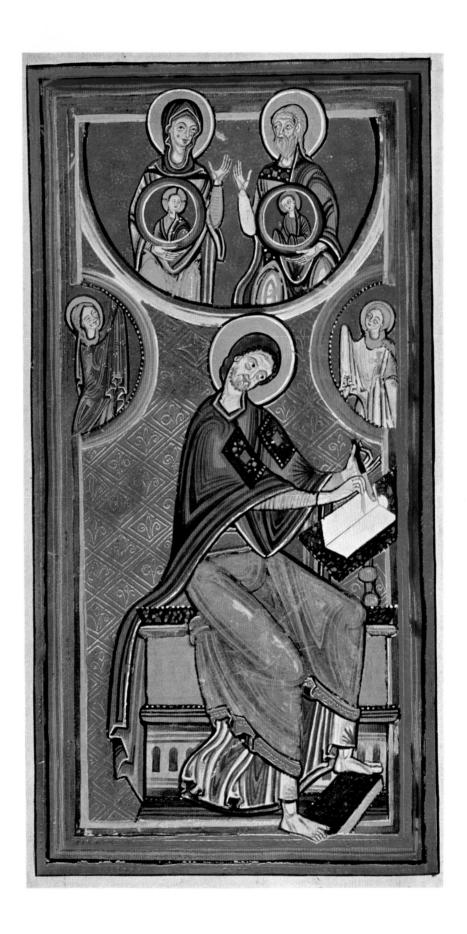

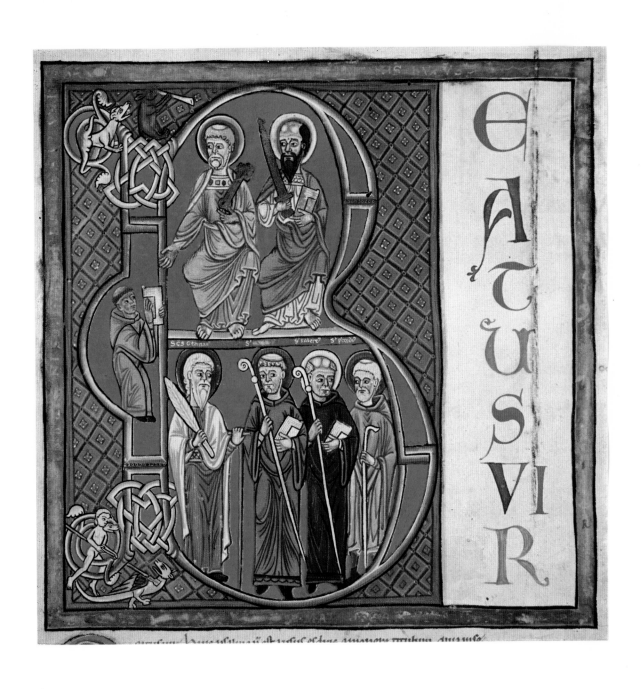

XXX – HERBERT DURSENS OFFERS HIS BOOK TO SS. PETER AND PAUL. Gilbert de la Porrée, *Commentaire des Psaumes;* Corbie, second half of the 12th century (Bibliothèque Nationale, Ms. lat. 12004, f. 1 v.)

XXXI – DECORATED INITIAL. Zacharias of Besançon, *Concordances;* Anchin, second half of the 12th century
(Douai, Ms. 42, f. 101)

XXXII – A SCENE FROM THE LIFE OF ST. AMANDUS. *Vie de saint Amand;* Saint-Amand, second half of the 12th century (Valenciennes, Ms. 500, f. 61)

XXXIV – ST. JOHN. *Gospel Book;* Liessies, second quarter of the 12th century (Avesnes, Société Archéologique)

XXXV – ST. AMANDUS AND BAUDEMUNDUS. *Vie de saint Amand*, second half of the 12th century (Valenciennes, Ms. 501, f. 58 v.)

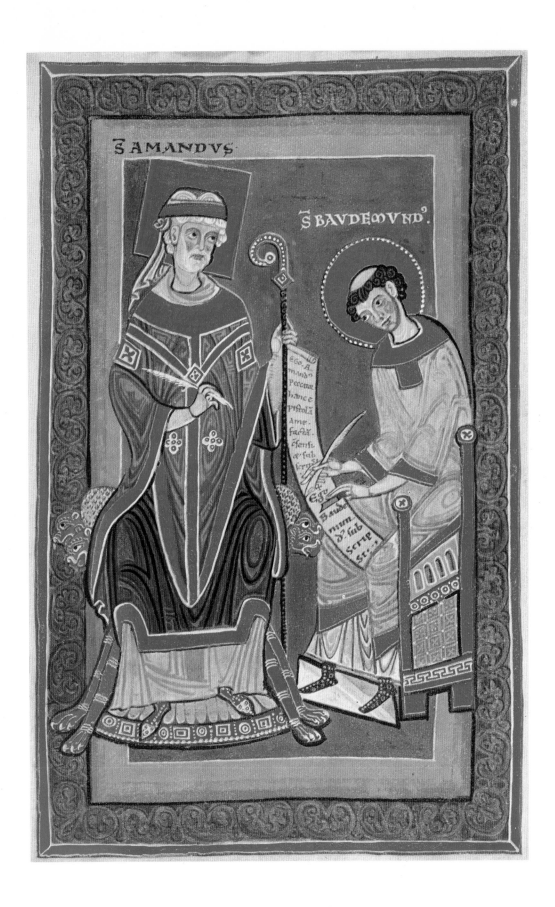

XXXVI – THE VIRGIN AND CHILD. *Bible*, second half of the 12th century (Lyons, Ms. 410, f. 207 v.)

XXXVII – THE DEPARTURE OF TOBIAS. *Bible*, second half of the 12th century (Clermont-Ferrand, Ms. 1, f. 203)

XXXVIII – THE ANNUNCIATION TO ZACHARIAS. *Bible*, second half of the 12th century
(Bibliothèque Nationale, Ms. lat. 16746, f. 42)

o.

omnia
tedictt
ticho

ruoz
suo de
rentur
u sui pro

domini.
tenentes
repellit.
ciat. a
rogatur.

Ne timeas zacharia qm graudita e oratio tua. & uxor tua elisabeth pariet t filium.

Vnde hoc sciam. Ego enim sum senex. & uxor mea processit in diebus suis.

Ecce eris tacens. & n poteris loqi usqi in diem quo hec fiunt.

VNDIAM QUIDEM : MULTI :
conati sunt ordinare narrationem
que in nobis complete sunt rerum.

XXXIX – ESTHER AND AHASUERUS. *Bible*, second half of the 12th century (Bibliothèque Nationale, Ms. lat. 116, f. 65)

& leuiticum; Igitur mundaui eos ab omnib;
alienigenis. & constitui ordines sacerdotum
& leuitarū. uniuquéq; in ministerio suo. &
in oblatione lignox. in téporib; constitutis
& in pmitiuis; Explicit LIBER EZRAE.

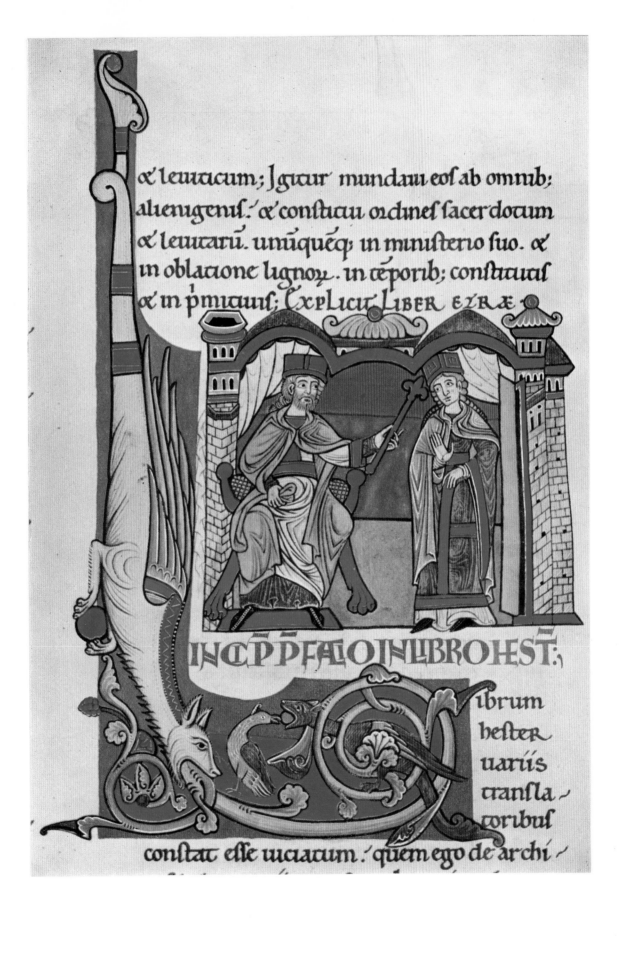

INCP PFALO IN LIBRO HEST;

ibrum
hester
uariis
transla-
toribus
constat esse uiciatum; quem ego de archi-

XLI – THE ENTOMBMENT: THE THREE MARYS AT THE SEPULCHRE. *The Ingeburga Psalter*, circa 1200–1205 (Chantilly, Musée Condé, Ms. 1695, f. 28 v.)

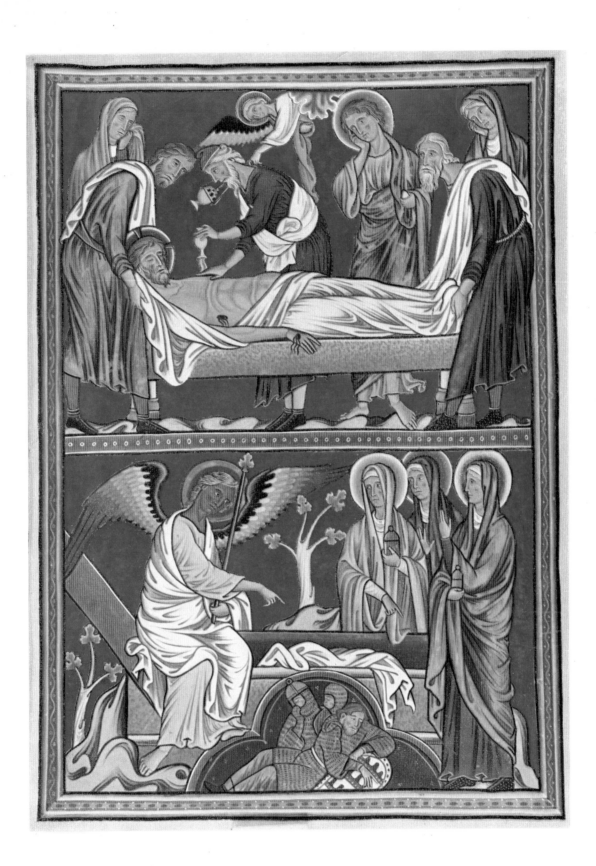

XLII – THE NATIVITY: THE ANNUNCIATION TO THE SHEPHERDS. *Paris Psalter*, circa 1230
(Bibliothèque de l'Arsenal, Ms. 1186, f. 17)

XLIII – ABRAHAM AND ELIEZER: REBECCA GIVES DRINK TO ELIEZER. *Psalter of St. Louis*, between 1253 and 1270
(Bibliothèque Nationale, Ms. lat. 10525, f. 12)

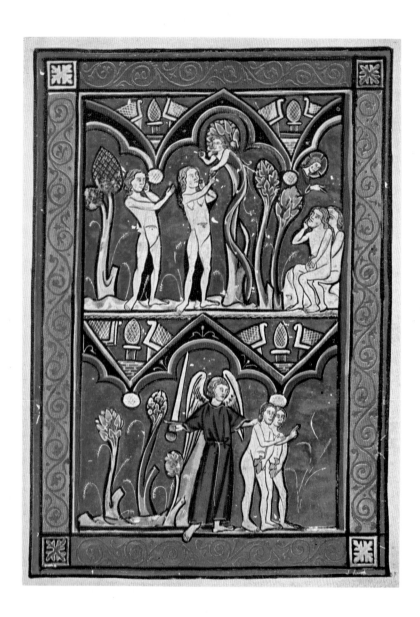

XLIV – THE STORY OF ADAM AND EVE. *Paris Psalter*, circa 1250 (Bibliothèque Nationale, Ms. lat. 10434, f. 10)

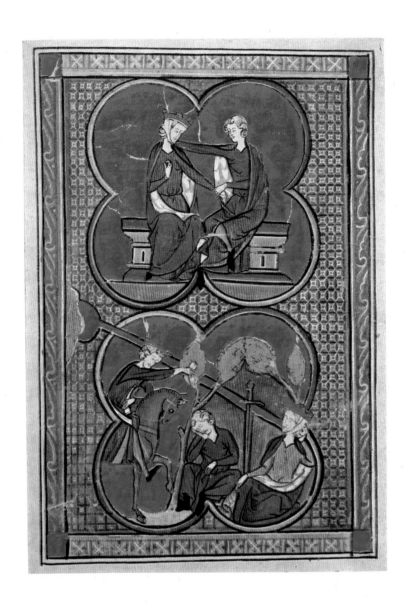

XLVI – TRISTAN AND ISOLDE SURPRISED BY KING MARK. *Roman de la Poire*, circa 1275
(Bibliothèque Nationale, Ms. fr. 2186, f. 5)

XLVII – THRESHING CORN. *Martyrologe de Saint-Germain-des-Prés*, circa 1270 (Bibliothèque Nationale, Ms. lat. 12834, f. 64 v.)

XLVIII – THE ANNOINTING OF DAVID: DAVID AND GOLIATH. *Breviary of Philip the Fair*, end of the 13th century
(Bibliothèque Nationale, Ms. lat. 1023, f. 1 v.)

Samuel. Yſai. Bethleem.

OBVID

Saul. Dauid. golias. Dauid

XLIX – KING LOT LEAVES QUEEN GUINIVERE'S CASTLE: BATTLE AGAINST THE SAXONS. Robert de Borron, *Histoire du Graal*, circa 1280 (Bibliothèque Nationale, Ms. fr. 95, f. 292 v.)

plains qui
si encontrent
menoient g
prisons loie
uentres des
iles (
et u
et j
uauchoit
qui ensi auo
tes que por
uatissent li
pur nelensu
ne les uirent
bien A lor an

Er dist li contes que quant
ce uint au premier somme
si se leua li rois loth et si uu

L – ST. DIONYSIUS PREACHING: THE CONVERSION OF LISBIUS. Yves, *Vie de saint Denis*, 1317
(Bibliothèque Nationale, Ms. fr. 2091, f. 99)

LI – THE ADORATION OF THE MAGI. *Arras Psalter and Hours,* circa 1300 (Bibliothèque Nationale, Ms. lat. 1328, f. 28)

LII – THE STORY OF THE EMPEROR HERACLIUS: PETER THE HERMIT. *Roman de Godefroi de Bouillon*, 1337
(Bibliothèque Nationale, Ms. fr. 22495, f. 9)

LIII – THE EMPRESS OF ROME. Gautier de Coincy, *Miracles de la Vierge*, circa 1330
(Bibliothèque Nationale, Ms. nouv. acq. fr. 24541, f. 119)

LIV – THE ANNUNCIATION. *Heures de Jeanne d'Évreux*, circa 1325 (New York, Cloisters Museum, f. 16)

spreuit eos. Quis dabit ex syon salutare israel. cum auerteret dominus captiuitatem plebis sue. exultabit iacob. letabitur israel. ps dauid

Deus in nomine tuo saluum me fac: et in uirtute tua iudica me. Deus exaudi orationem meam: auribus percipe uerba oris mei. Quoniam alieni insurrexerunt aduersum me: et fortes quesierunt animam meam: et non proposuerunt deum ante conspectum suum. Ecce enim deus adiuuat me: et dominus susceptor est anime mee. Auerte mala inimicis meis: et in ueritate tua disperde illos. Voluntarie sacrificabo tibi et confitebor nomini tuo domine quoniam bonum est: Quoniam ex omni tribulatione eripuisti me: et super inimicos meos despexit oculus meus. ps dauid Exaudi deus orationem meam et ne despexeris deprecationem meam: intende michi et exaudi me. Contristatus sum in exercitatione me

Dixit insipiens in corde suo: non est deus. Corrupti sunt et abhominabiles facti sunt: in iniquitatibus: non est qui faciat bonum. Dominus de celo prospexit super filios hominum: ut uideat si est intelligens aut requirens deum. Omnes declinauerunt simul inutiles facti sunt: non est qui faciat bonum non est usque ad unum. Nonne scient omnes qui operantur iniquitatem: qui deuorant plebem meam ut cibum panis. Deum non inuocauerunt illic trepidauerunt timore: ubi non fuit timor. Quoniam deus dissipauit ossa eorum qui hominibus placent: confusi sunt quoniam deus

Côment nature voulant ozendroit plus
que onques mes reuele z faire essaucier
les biens z honneurs qui sont en amours
vient a Guillē de machaut z li ozdene z en
charge afaire sur ce nouueaur dis amou

I nature par qui tout est fourme
quanque a cams z sur tere z en mer
uyeng et a toy Guillē qui fourme
ay a part pour faire par toy fourmer
Li honneurs des amoureur plaisans

QV COMENCENT LES PABOL

TV commencent les paraboles Salomon   trespassons et les saages et les mauu

LIX – ST. AUGUSTINE OFFERS HIS BOOK TO THE LORD: THE SACK OF ROME BY THE GOTHS. St. Augustine, *Cité de Dieu*, circa 1410 (Bibliothèque Nationale, Ms. fr. 25, f. 5)

Egote · xxv ·

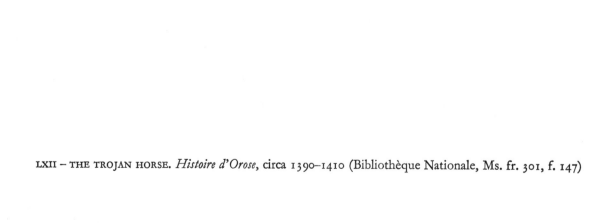

LXII – THE TROJAN HORSE. *Histoire d'Orose*, circa 1390–1410 (Bibliothèque Nationale, Ms. fr. 301, f. 147)

LXIII – THE PROPHET ISAIAH. *Psalter of Jean de Berry*, circa 1380–1385 (Bibliothèque Nationale, Ms. fr. 13091, f. 11 v.)

LXIV – THE NATIVITY. *Petites Heures de Jean de Berry*, circa 1390 (Bibliothèque Nationale, Ms. lat. 18014, f. 58)

eus in adiutorium meum in
tende Domine ad adiuuandu
me festina. Gloria pri. Sicut
erat. hympnus.

eni creator spe mentes tuorum visi
ta imple supna gra que tu creasti pre

LXV – ABRAHAM AND HIS WIFE DEPART FROM EGYPT. *Bible of Jean de Cis*, circa 1390
(Bibliothèque Nationale, Ms. fr. 15 397, f. 14)

scendit ergo   abram sen monta de

abram. et ecc.   egipte lui et sa femme

Quant au p   et toutes les choses q̃ il

LXVII – THE MARRIAGE AT CANA: DISTRIBUTION TO THE POOR. *Grandes Heures de Jean de Berry*, 1409
(Bibliothèque Nationale, Ms. lat. 919, f. 41)

ulfzquo d
an a mc.

Quan
lilia ui a
m odd m

lfpt
muinais
fpiet ct u
us meu

onucre nos de
us faluraris nr
t aucrte tra

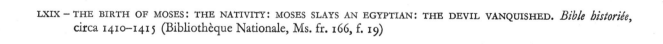

LXIX – THE BIRTH OF MOSES: THE NATIVITY: MOSES SLAYS AN EGYPTIAN: THE DEVIL VANQUISHED. *Bible historiée*, circa 1410–1415 (Bibliothèque Nationale, Ms. fr. 166, f. 19)

LXX – JEAN DE BERRY SETS OUT ON A JOURNEY. *Petites Heures de Jean de Berry*, circa 1415
(Bibliothèque Nationale, Ms. lat. 18014, f. 288)

LXXI – THE CORONATION OF THE VIRGIN. *Très Riches Heures de Jean de Berry*, circa 1414–1416 (Chantilly, Musée Condé)

LXXII – THE LEGEND OF ST. GEORGE. *Bedford Breviary*, circa 1424–1435 (Bibliothèque Nationale, Ms. lat. 17 294, f. 447 v.)

puincia huc aduenisti: vel quo
nomine voceris. Sanctus ge
orgius dixit. Xpianus et dei
seruus sum: georgius nuncu
por gentre capadocus prie mee
comitatum gerens. Elegi vero
remporali carere dignitate: et

imortalis dei impio deseruire. se in
acianus dixit. Erras
georgi: accede et im
mola deo apollini.
Beatus georgius respondit. Do
mino ihesu xpisto exhibeo culti
ram omni seculox: non appol

LXXIII – a, b. SCENES FROM THE "EUNUCHUS" AND "HECYRA". *Térence des Ducs*, circa 1405–1410
(Bibliothèque de l'Arsenal, Ms. 664, ff. 47, 75 v.)

LXXIII – c, d. SCENES FROM THE "EUNUCHUS" AND "HECYRA". *Térence des Ducs*, circa 1405–1410
(Bibliothèque de l'Arsenal, Ms. 664, ff. 85 v., 209 v.)

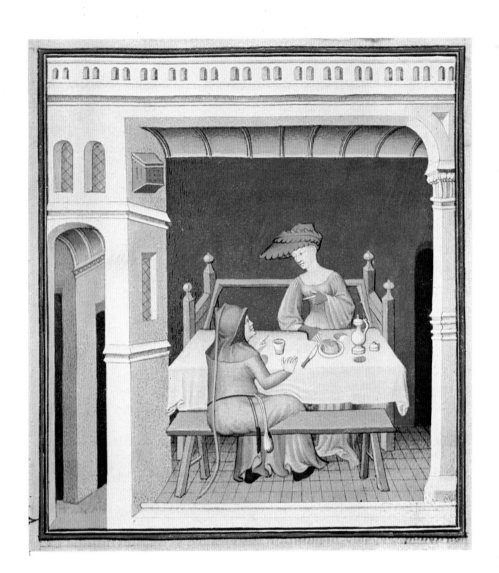

LXXIV – GASTON DE FOIX ISSUES ORDERS TO HIS HUNTSMEN. Gaston Phébus, *Livre de la chasse*, circa 1405–1410 (Bibliothèque Nationale, Ms. fr. 616, f. 13)

LXXV – JOHN THE FEARLESS, DUKE OF BURGUNDY, RECEIVES A PRESENTATION COPY OF HAYTON'S TRAVELS. *Livre des merveilles*, circa 1410 (Bibliothèque Nationale, Ms. fr. 2810, f. 226)

Cy commence le liure frere Jehan hayton de lordre de pre monstre tousm
gernem du roy darmenie qui parle des merueilles. des .xiiij. roiaulmes dasie

LXXVI – THE ANNUNCIATION. *Heures de Paris*, circa 1410 (Bibliothèque Nationale, Ms. lat. 1161, f. 31)

LXXVII – A DEAD MAN FACE TO FACE WITH HIS JUDGE. *Heures de Rohan*, circa 1418–1425
(Bibliothèque Nationale, Ms. lat. 9471, f. 159)

LXXX – THE BIRTH OF ST. JOHN THE BAPTIST. *Heures d'Étienne Chevalier*, circa 1450 (Chantilly, Musée Condé)

LXXXI – a. KING GONTRAN SURRENDERS THE KINGDOM TO HIS NEPHEW CHILDEBERT BEFORE ORLEANS. *Grandes Chroniques de France*, circa 1460 (Bibliothèque Nationale, Ms. fr. 6465, f. 45 v.)

LXXXI – b. EDWARD II OF ENGLAND DOES HOMAGE TO PHILIP THE FAIR FOR AQUITAINE. *Grandes Chroniques de France*, circa 1460 (Bibliothèque Nationale, Ms. fr. 6465, f. 301 v.)

LXXXII – THE VISITATION. *Heures de Rome*, circa 1450 (Bibliothèque Nationale, Ms. Rothschild 2530, f. 45)

LXXXIII – LOVE AND FORTUNE. *Chansonnier de Jean de Montchenu,* circa 1460–1476
(Bibliothèque Nationale, Ms. Rothschild 2973, f. 1)

LXXXIV – THE KING OF ARMS PRESENTS EIGHT COATS TO THE DUKE OF BOURBON, René of Anjou, *Le Livre des Tournois,* circa 1460–1465 (Bibliothèque Nationale, Ms. fr. 2695, f. 11)

LXXXVII – THE VIRGIN OF PITY. *Heures d'Anne de Bretagne*, circa 1500–1508 (Bibliothèque Nationale, Ms. lat. 9474, f. 3)

LXXXVIII – MARGARET OF AUSTRIA(?). End of the 15th century (Bibliothèque Nationale, Ms. lat. 1190)

LXXXIX – THE AUTHOR TAKES DÉSIRÉ INTO THE ORCHARD. *Les Échecs amoureux*, circa 1500
(Bibliothèque Nationale, Ms. fr. 143, f. 198 v.)

uant dyane se fut   de sa follye sicõe il famt en
partie de lacte² des³   son snux il lessa la forest
dit et glle lot repris   ou dyane comerse ² trau

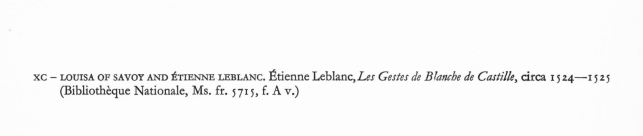

XC – LOUISA OF SAVOY AND ÉTIENNE LEBLANC. Étienne Leblanc, *Les Gestes de Blanche de Castille*, circa 1524—1525 (Bibliothèque Nationale, Ms. fr. 5715, f. A v.)

LIST OF ILLUSTRATIONS

XIX THE HISTORIAN JOSEPHUS. Flavius Josephus, *De Bello Judaico;* Toulouse, end of the 11th century (Bibliothèque Nationale, Ms. lat. 5058, f. 3)

XX ST. ALBINUS BLESSES THE BREAD AND WINE. *Vie de saint Aubin;* Angers, end of the 11th century (Bibliothèque Nationale, Ms. nouv. acq. lat. 1390, f. 2)

XXI A SCENE FROM THE LIFE OF ST. AUDOMARUS. *Vie de saint Omer,* end of the 11th century (Saint-Omer, Ms. 698, f. 34)

XXII ST. MARK. *Gospel Book;* Corbie, end of the 11th century (Amiens, Ms. 24, f. 53)

XXIII THE MASTER AND HIS SERVANT. *Lectionary of Rheims Cathedral,* end of the 11th century (Rheims, Ms. 294, f. 191)

XXIV DANIEL IN THE LIONS' DEN. St. Jerome, *Explanatio in Prophetas;* Cîteaux, first half of the 12th century (Dijon, Ms. 132, f. 2)

XXV THE VIRGIN AND CHILD. St. Jerome, *Explanatio in Isaiam;* Cîteaux, first half of the 12th century (Dijon, Ms. 129, f. 4)

XXVI GOD CALLS JUDAS TO SUCCEED JOSHUA. *Bible of Saint-Martial, Limoges,* end of the 11th century (Bibliothèque Nationale, Ms. lat. 8, Vol. 1, f. 91)

XXVII THE SOUL OF LAMBERT, ABBOT OF SAINT-BERTIN, ASCENDS TO GOD. Saint-Bertin, circa 1125 (Boulogne, Ms. 46, f. 1)

XXVIII BISHOP FRECULF: RABANUS MAURUS WITH HIS PUPILS. Rabanus Maurus, *Commentary on Exodus;* Anchin, second half of the 12th century (Douai, Ms. 339, f. 2 v.)

XXIX ST. MATTHEW. *Gospel Book of Hénin-Liétard;* Saint-Bertin, middle of the 12th century (Boulogne, Ms. 14, Vol. 1, f. 22 v.)

XXX HERBERT DURSENS OFFERS HIS BOOK TO SS. PETER AND PAUL. Gilbert de la Porrée, *Commentaire des Psaumes;* Corbie, second half of the 12th century (Bibliothèque Nationale, Ms. lat. 12004, f. 1 v.)

XXXI DECORATED INITIAL. Zacharias of Besançon, *Concordances;* Anchin, second half of the 12th century (Douai, Ms. 42, f. 101)

XXXII A SCENE FROM THE LIFE OF ST. AMANDUS. *Vie de saint Amand;* Saint-Amand, second half of the 12th century (Valenciennes, Ms. 500, f. 61)

XXXIII ST. GREGORY. *Lettres de saint Grégoire;* Saint-Amand, second half of the 12th century (Bibliothèque Nationale, Ms. lat. 2287, f. 1 v.)

XXXIV ST. JOHN. *Gospel Book;* Liessies, second quarter of the 12th century (Avesnes, Société Archéologique)

XXXV ST. AMANDUS AND BAUDEMUNDUS. *Vie de saint Amand,* second half of the 12th century (Valenciennes, Ms. 501, f. 58 v.)

XXXVI THE VIRGIN AND CHILD. *Bible,* second half of the 12th century (Lyons, Ms. 410, f. 207 v.)

XXXVII THE DEPARTURE OF TOBIAS. *Bible,* second half of the 12th century (Clermont-Ferrand, Ms. 1, f. 203)

XXXVIII THE ANNUNCIATION TO ZACHARIAS. *Bible,* second half of the 12th century (Bibliothèque Nationale, Ms. lat. 16746, f. 42)

XXXIX ESTHER AND AHASUERUS. *Bible,* second half of the 12th century (Bibliothèque Nationale, Ms. lat. 116, f. 65)

XL SCENES FROM THE BIBLE. *Bible moralisée,* circa 1250 (Bibliothèque Nationale, Ms. lat. 11560, f. 128)

XLI THE ENTOMBMENT: THE THREE MARYS AT THE SEPULCHRE. *The Ingeburga Psalter,* circa 1200–1205 (Chantilly, Musée Condé, Ms. 1695, f. 28 v.)

XLII THE NATIVITY: THE ANNUNCIATION TO THE SHEPHERDS. *Paris Psalter,* circa 1230 (Bibliothèque de l'Arsenal, Ms. 1186, f. 17)

XLIII ABRAHAM AND ELIEZER: REBECCA GIVES DRINK TO ELIEZER. *Psalter of St. Louis,* between 1253 and 1270 (Bibliothèque Nationale, Ms. lat. 10525, f. 12)

XLIV THE STORY OF ADAM AND EVE. *Paris Psalter,* circa 1250 (Bibliothèque Nationale, Ms. lat. 10434, f. 10)

XLV SCENES FROM THE APOCALYPSE. Lambert de Saint-Omer, *Liber Floridus,* circa 1260 (Bibliothèque Nationale, Ms. lat. 8865, f. 39)

XLVI TRISTAN AND ISOLDE SURPRISED BY KING MARK. *Roman de la Poire,* circa 1275 (Bibliothèque Nationale, Ms. fr. 2186, f. 5)

XLVII   THRESHING CORN. *Martyrologe de Saint-Germain-des-Prés*, circa 1270 (Bibliothèque Nationale, Ms. lat. 12834, f. 64 v.)

XLVIII   THE ANOINTING OF DAVID: DAVID AND GOLIATH. *Breviary of Philip the Fair*, end of the 13th century (Bibliothèque Nationale, Ms. lat. 1023, f. 1 v.)

XLIX   KING LOT LEAVES QUEEN GUINIVERE'S CASTLE: BATTLE AGAINST THE SAXONS. Robert de Borron, *Histoire du Graal*, circa 1280 (Bibliothèque Nationale, Ms. fr. 95, f. 292 v.)

L   ST. DIONYSIUS PREACHING: THE CONVERSION OF LISBIUS. Yves, *Vie de saint Denis*, 1317 (Bibliothèque Nationale, Ms. fr. 2091, f. 99)

LI   THE ADORATION OF THE MAGI. *Arras Psalter and Hours*, circa 1300 (Bibliothèque Nationale, Ms. lat. 1328, f. 28)

LII   THE STORY OF THE EMPEROR HERACLIUS: PETER THE HERMIT. *Roman de Godefroi de Bouillon*, 1337 (Bibliothèque Nationale, Ms. fr. 22495, f. 9)

LIII   THE EMPRESS OF ROME. Gautier de Coincy, *Miracles de la Vierge*, circa 1330 (Bibliothèque Nationale, Ms. nouv. acq. fr. 24541, f. 119)

LIV   THE ANNUNCIATION. *Heures de Jeanne d'Évreux*, circa 1325 (New York, Cloisters Museum, f. 16)

LV   THE DEATH OF ABSALOM: A KING DETHRONED, THE SACRAMENT OF ORDINATION, THE GIFT OF INTELLIGENCE. *Breviary of Charles V*, second half of the 14th century (Bibliothèque Nationale, Ms. lat. 1052, f. 232)

LVI   NATURE PRESENTS TO GUILLAUME DE MACHAUT HER CHILDREN: SENSE, RHETORIC AND MUSIC. *Oeuvres de Guillaume de Machaut*, circa 1370 (Bibliothèque Nationale, Ms. fr. 1584, f. E)

LVII   THE CORONATION OF CHARLES VI. *Grandes Chroniques de France*, circa 1375–1379 (Bibliothèque Nationale, Ms. fr. 2813, f. 3 v.)

LVIII   SCENES FROM THE LIFE OF SOLOMON. Guiart des Moulins, *Bible historiale*, circa 1400–1402 (Bibliothèque Nationale, Ms. fr. 159, f. 289 v.)

LIX   ST. AUGUSTINE OFFERS HIS BOOK TO THE LORD: THE SACK OF ROME BY THE GOTHS. St. Augustine, *Cité de Dieu*, circa 1410 (Bibliothèque Nationale, Ms. fr. 25, f. 5)

LX   THE HEBREWS IN THE DESERT. Flavius Josephus, *Antiquités judaïques*, circa 1410 (Bibliothèque Nationale, Ms. fr. 247, f. 49)

LXI   ULYSSES BLINDS THE CYCLOPS. Christine de Pisan, *Épître d'Othéa à Hector*, circa 1400–1402 (Bibliothèque Nationale, Ms. fr. 606, f. 11)

LXII   THE TROJAN HORSE. *Histoire d'Orose*, circa 1390–1410 (Bibliothèque Nationale, Ms. fr. 301, f. 147)

LXIII   THE PROPHET ISAIAH. *Psalter of Jean de Berry*, circa 1380–1385 (Bibliothèque Nationale, Ms. fr. 13091, f. 11 v.)

LXIV   THE NATIVITY. *Petites Heures de Jean de Berry*, circa 1390 (Bibliothèque Nationale, Ms. lat. 18014, f. 58)

LXV   ABRAHAM AND HIS WIFE DEPART FROM EGYPT. *Bible of Jean de Cis*, circa 1390 (Bibliothèque Nationale, Ms. fr. 15397, f. 14)

LXVI   THE NATIVITY. *Très Belles Heures de Jean de Berry*, circa 1400–1407 (Bibliothèque Nationale, Ms. nouv. acq. lat. 3093, f. 42)

LXVII   THE MARRIAGE AT CANA: DISTRIBUTION TO THE POOR. *Grandes Heures de Jean de Berry*, 1409 (Bibliothèque Nationale, Ms. lat. 919, f. 41)

LXVIII   THE ADORATION OF THE MAGI. *Belles Heures de Jean de Berry*, circa 1410–1413 (New York, Cloisters Museum, f. 48 v.)

LXIX   THE BIRTH OF MOSES: THE NATIVITY: MOSES SLAYS AN EGYPTIAN: THE DEVIL VANQUISHED. *Bible historiée*, circa 1410–1415 (Bibliothèque Nationale, Ms. fr. 166, f. 19)

LXX   JEAN DE BERRY SETS OUT ON A JOURNEY. *Petites Heures de Jean de Berry*, circa 1415 (Bibliothèque Nationale, Ms. lat. 18014, f. 288)

LXXI   THE CORONATION OF THE VIRGIN. *Très Riches Heures de Jean de Berry*, circa 1414–1416 (Chantilly, Musée Condé)

LXXII   THE LEGEND OF ST. GEORGE. *Bedford Breviary*, circa 1424–1435 (Bibliothèque Nationale, Ms. lat. 17294, f. 447 v.)

LXXIII   a, b. SCENES FROM THE "EUNUCHUS" AND "HECYRA". *Térence des Ducs*, circa 1405–1410 (Bibliothèque de l'Arsenal, Ms. 664, ff. 47, 75 v.)
         c, d. SCENES FROM THE "EUNUCHUS" AND "HECYRA". *Térence des Ducs*, circa 1405–1410 (Bibliothèque de l'Arsenal, Ms. 664, ff. 85 v., 209 v.)

Photographs

All the colour photographs were taken specially for this book, except Pls. LIV and LXVIII, which are from the Cloisters Museum, New York.

All the black-and-white photographs are from the Bibliothèque Nationale, except the following:

Archives Photographiques (Fig. 27); Biblioteca Apostolica Vaticana (Fig. 4); Bamberg, Staatsbibliothek (Fig. 9); London, British Museum (Fig. 6); Giraudon (Figs. 67, 68, 79, 80, 81); Anderson (Fig. 29); Saint-Germain, Hurault (Fig. 28); Sheffield, Ruskin Museum (Fig. 82).

INDEX

Italic numbers refer to pages